# AWARD-WINNING QUICK QUILTS

JUDY FLORENCE

Other books by Judy Florence:

*Award-Winning Quilts and How to Make Them*
*Award-Winning Quilts, Book* II
*Award-Winning Scrap Quilts*

Cover design and interior layout: Anthony Jacobson
Editor: Jill Champion
Photographs: Jim Christoffersen

Library of Congress Catalog Card Number 87-51439

ISBN 0-87069-508-8

10 9 8 7 6 5 4 3 2

Published by

A Capital Cities/ABC, Inc. Company

Wallace-Homestead Book Company
201 King of Prussia Road
Radnor, Pennsylvania 19089

To
Pat Simonsen, Ann Ohl, and Dorothy Gilbertson
with gratitude
for their friendship and encouragement.

# Contents

Preface . . . . . . . . . . . . . . . . . . . . . . . . . . . . . . . . . . . . . . . . . vii
Acknowledgments . . . . . . . . . . . . . . . . . . . . . . . . . . . . . . . . vii
Introduction . . . . . . . . . . . . . . . . . . . . . . . . . . . . . . . . . . . . ix

**Part I: Quilts Based on Tandem-Pieced Triangles**   1

*Chapters*
1. Four-Patch Sampler . . . . . . . . . . . . . . . . . . . . . . . 3
2. Ships . . . . . . . . . . . . . . . . . . . . . . . . . . . . . . . . . 11
3. Nine-Patch Churn Dash . . . . . . . . . . . . . . . . 19
4. Pieced Star Wall Quilt . . . . . . . . . . . . . . . . . . 35
5. Dorothy's Dilemma . . . . . . . . . . . . . . . . . . . . 41

**Part II: Other Quick Quilts** . . . . . . . . . . . . . . . 49

*Chapters*
6. Sweet Dreams Crib Quilt . . . . . . . . . . . . . . . 51
7. Holiday Quick Quilt . . . . . . . . . . . . . . . . . . . 57
8. Bow Tie Wall Quilt . . . . . . . . . . . . . . . . . . . . 63
9. Computer Symmetry . . . . . . . . . . . . . . . . . . 69
10. Little Red Schoolhouse . . . . . . . . . . . . . . . . 75

Appendix: How to Make Tandem-Pieced Triangles   87
Bibliography . . . . . . . . . . . . . . . . . . . . . . . . . . . . . . 93
About the Author . . . . . . . . . . . . . . . . . . . . . . . . . . 94

# Preface

Award-Winning Quick Quilts is the fourth title in a series of books featuring innovative quilt patterns. This book concentrates on quilts that include one or more *quick* or *efficient* methods of marking, cutting, and piecing. Complete directions for ten quilts are included; these quilts were chosen for their adaptability to quick techniques as well as for their variety and beauty.

You can select your own level of commitment from among the patterns in this book because both large and small projects are covered: There are two crib quilts, four wall quilts, and four bed quilts. While some are embarrassingly quick, others feature rapid cutting or piecing, but require additional time for quilting—an attractive feature for the quiltmaker who favors quilting over piecing. A bonus feature of *Award-Winning Quick Quilts* is the inclusion of more than 25 designs for hand-quilting.

Five of the featured quilts are made with tandem-pieced triangles, and the other five employ various other quick methods such as strip-piecing or multiple-layer cutting.

Three quilts include more traditional template piecing for those who favor that method. Those quilts are small in size and have an attractive variety of fabrics and quilting designs. The innovative ''quick-piecer'' will be able to apply newer streamlined techniques to these projects. Some tips are included.

## Acknowledgments

Some of the quilts included in *Award-Winning Quick Quilts* were created by special quilting friends. Thanks to Pat Simonsen for her attractive Little Red Schoolhouse, which she adapted from traditional schoolhouse patterns. Thanks to Ann Ohl for the confidence to take an image from my computer and transform it into the fabric of her Computer Symmetry quilt. Thanks to Dorothy Gilbertson for her willingness to explore tandem-piecing methods in her Dorothy's Dilemma.

I am also grateful to Marie Halmstad for her Nine-Patch Churn Dash and to Marky Kuba for her Pieced Star.

I have known these five quiltmakers for several years. All have been students of mine. All have become enduring friends. I thank them for their dedication to quilting and their willingness to share.

# Introduction

The patterns and techniques in *Award-Winning Quick Quilts* assume a general knowledge of basic piecing and quilting skills, although they are suitable for experienced *and* beginning needleworkers. Since this book is designed to complement the other books in the Award-Winning series, basic quilting how-tos have not been repeated from the three previous books. For those wishing to learn or freshen up on the basics, I have included a list of recommended reading material later in this section.

## Chapters

There are ten chapters in this book, each covering one of the ten different quick quilts pictured in the color photo section. Each chapter is divided into six sections as follows:

*Remarks.* Brief overview of the quilt design and various methods used.

*For Starters.* List of tips and general information about the quilt, including dimensions.

*Supplies.* Fabric types and sizes for the different parts of the quilt, along with a list of necessary quilting tools and supplies.

*Ready to Work.* Color key and instructions for cutting and piecing fabrics.

*Putting It Together.* Instructions for assembling the quilt top, latticework, and borders.

*The Finished Product.* Instructions for quilting and finishing.

The Appendix, "How to Make Tandem-Pieced Triangles," covers the details of seam allowances, marking intervals, and stitching intervals, and gives step-by-step instructions for making tandem-pieced triangles, which are used for the first five quilts.

## References

Several good references for quick quilt-making methods and patterns can be found in the bibliography. Several authors have explored quick-piecing methods, and new procedures are continuously being both discovered and applied to quiltmaking. Some authors give specific tips for tandem piecing, strip-piecing, and piecing without templates.

The tandem-piecing method (half-square triangles) is illustrated and explained in several of the reference books. Barbara Johannah's 1979 publication, *Quick Quiltmaking Handbook*, covers many basic quick-piecing methods, including tandem piecing. I have used this book as a recommended text in quick-quiltmaking classes for several semesters; it is reasonably priced and still available.

Johannah has expanded on the tandem-piecing technique in her new book, *Half Square Triangles*, a comprehensive study of pattern discovery and formation.

I recommend *Award-Winning Quilts and How to Make Them* (the first book in my series) for some of the basics such as elementary piecing, preparing for quilting, and making binding. The book also contains patterns that can be converted easily into "quick-pieced" patterns.

*Award-Winning Quilts, Book II* includes two computer patterns featuring streamlined cutting and piecing that are similar to the Computer Symmetry pattern in this book.

*Award-Winning Scrap Quilts* (the third book) contains patterns with quick-piecing potential as well, plus a Bow Tie–design section that complements the Bow Tie Wall Quilt included in this book.

All four books are available through Wallace-Homestead Book Company.

# Part I
# Quilts Based on
# Tandem-Pieced
# Triangles

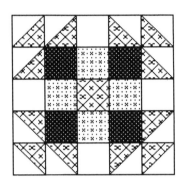

# Chapter 1
# Four-Patch Sampler

Quilt by the author

## Remarks

The designs in Four-Patch Sampler are based on the traditional double–four-patch (16 units in each block pattern). Twelve different designs are included in the instructions. Some are traditional and recognizable, others more innovative, and all are easy to assemble. You can easily add or create your own double four-patch variations to include in your quilt. Think of these 12 designs as suggestions or guidelines.

The graphic effect of Four-Patch Sampler is based on the mixture and placement of three blue fabrics—a light, a medium, and a dark. Fabric selection within this monochromatic theme should be trouble-free, and you can easily change to any color range of your choice.

Before you begin cutting the fabric, read through all the instructions *and* the appendix, ''How to Make Tandem-Pieced Triangles.''

## For Starters

- Wash and press all fabrics before you begin.
- Four-Patch Sampler requires only three fabrics—a light blue, a medium blue, and a dark blue.
- The marking unit for the tandem-pieced triangles is a 6" square.
- The paired triangle units measure 4¼" square when finished.
- The finished blocks (a total of 12) measure 17" square.
- The latticework/border pieces measure 3" wide.
- The seam width is ½".
- The finished size for Four-Patch Sampler is 63" × 83", adequate for a twin bed.

## Supplies

### Quilt Top Fabric
Use 44"/45"–wide cotton or cotton/polyester blends.

| | |
|---|---|
| Light print | 3¼ yards (for blocks) |
| Medium print | 2½ yards (for latticework/borders) |
| Dark print | 3¼ yards (for blocks) |

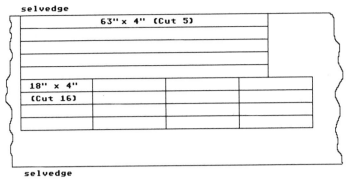

selvedge

63" x 4" (Cut 5)

18" x 4"
(Cut 16)

selvedge

**Diagram 1-1. Layout for Medium Print (M)**

## Backing
Requires 5½ yards of unbleached muslin.

## Binding
Use 1 yard of dark blue fabric.

## Batting
Use a 72" X 90" (twin size) piece of bonded polyester.

## Other Supplies
• Regular sewing thread to match the fabrics
• A sewing machine
• A long straightedge
• A pencil
• Two spools of natural-color quilting thread
• Thread or safety pins for basting
• Soap chips or marking pencils
• Pins and quilting needles
• A large right triangle or T-square
• Scissors
• A quilting hoop or frame
• Optional: A rotary cutter and cutting mat

# Ready to Work

## Color Key
L   Light print
M   Medium print
D   Dark print

## Cutting
Begin with the light print (L). Cut three large pieces, each approximately 1 yard long. Each piece will measure about 36" X 45" and will be used for tandem piecing.

Next, cut three pieces, each approximately 1 yard long, from the dark print (D). These will be about the same size as the light-print pieces and will also be used for tandem piecing.

From the medium print (M), cut the following latticework/borders, according to Diagram 1-1:

• 5 cross-lattices, 63" X 4" (½" seam allowances included)
• 16 short strips, 18" X 4" (½" seam allowances included)

## Tandem Piecing
Begin with a 36" X 45" piece of light print (L). On the wrong side of the fabric, mark a grid of 6" squares (5 squares across, 7 squares down) for a total of 35 squares, according to Diagram 1-2. Mark diagonal lines as shown.

**Diagram 1-2. Marking Grid for Light Print (L)**

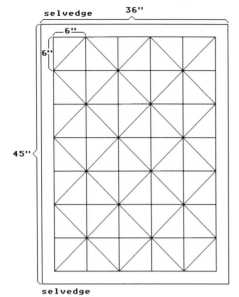

*Mark on **wrong** side of the fabric.*

Pin this piece to a 36" × 45" piece of dark print (D) with the right sides together. Stitch into tandem-pieced triangles using ½" seams. Use the suggested continuous lines and directional arrows given in Diagram 1-3 for the most efficient results.

**Diagram 1-3. Stitching Lines (½")**

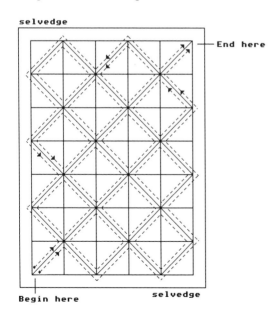

Refer to the Appendix, "How to Make Tandem-Pieced Triangles," for additional pointers.

Cut into squares, and then triangles. Press the seams toward the dark fabric. Trim each combination unit. You should have 70 L/D pieced units like the one shown in Diagram 1-4.

**Diagram 1-4. Four-Patch Sampler L/D Unit**

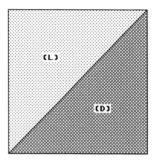

*You need 192 of these units.*

Mark the two remaining 36" × 45" light pieces in a similar way; then stitch, cut, press, and trim the additional L/D units. You'll need a total of 96 marked squares to get 192 combination units. You may have extras, depending on your fabric width and the number of 6" squares you can mark on each 45" width of fabric.

# Putting It Together

**Assembly of Blocks**
There are 12 different block designs in the Four-Patch Sampler; each consists of 16 paired-triangle units. Gather 16 units and lay them right sides up to complete each design. The 12 designs, 1-A through 1-L, are shown at the end of this chapter. You may alter or add to these designs at your discretion.

The piecing arrangement for Design 1-A is given in Diagram 1-5. Piece row 1 using short vertical ½" seams, as shown in Diagram 1-6. Piece rows 2, 3, and 4 in the same fashion.

5

**Diagram 1-5. Piecing Arrangement for Design 1-A**

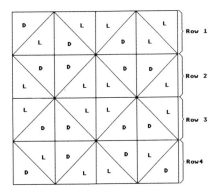

**Diagram 1-6. Piecing Row 1 for Design 1-A**

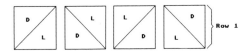

Press the seams of rows 1 and 3 to one side. Press the seams of rows 2 and 4 in the opposite direction. Join the four rows in horizontal seams, being careful to "butterfly" the seams at the intersections in order to minimize bulk. This will occur naturally if the rows are pressed as directed above. Press all cross-seams to one side.

Use similar piecing procedures for the 11 remaining designs, 1-B through 1-L (shown at the end of this chapter).

**Assembly of Quilt Top**

To assemble the top row of the quilt, gather four short lattice strips and three pieced blocks (Designs 1-A, 1-B, and 1-C). Arrange and stitch according to Diagram 1-7, using ½" seams. Similarly, piece the other three rows as shown in Diagram 1-8.

**Diagram 1-7. Top Row of Four-Patch Sampler**

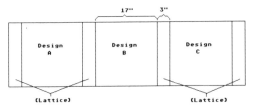

**Diagram 1-8. Four-Patch Sampler Layout**

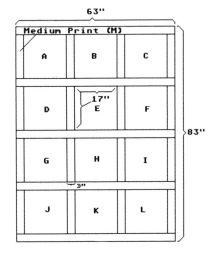

Add the long cross-lattices between each pieced row to complete the quilt top. Be careful to match the vertical lattices for accurate lines up and down the quilt.

# The Finished Product

**Quilting**

Cut the 5½-yard piece of unbleached muslin backing fabric into two 2¾-yard lengths, leaving one length intact. From the other length, cut two 15" panels and stitch these to each side of the intact panel. Press the seams to the outside.

Place the backing right side down. Smooth the batting over it. Place the pressed quilt top over the batting, right side up. Pin or baste the three layers together for quilting.

With a straightedge and soap chip or marking pencil, mark quilting lines ½" from the edge and "in the ditch" around each design unit. Suggested quilting lines for one of the blocks is given in Diagram 1-9. Suggested quilting for the latticework/borders is also given in Diagram 1-9.

**Diagram 1-9. Suggested Quilting for Design 1-A**

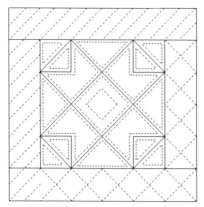

*Diagram is not to scale.*

## Finishing

Trim the batting to ½" larger than the quilt top to allow for filler in the binding. Trim the backing to match the top.

Make 3"-wide continuous bias binding from the 1 yard of dark blue fabric. For a finished binding of about ½", fold the binding—wrong sides together—and attach it to the quilt front, making sure the seam goes through all five layers. Turn the binding to the back of the quilt and whipstitch it in place.

**Design 1-A**

**Design 1-B**

**Design 1-C**

**Design 1-D**

**Design 1-E**

**Design 1-H**

**Design 1-F**

**Design 1-I**

**Design 1-G**

**Design 1-J**

**Design 1-K**

**Design 1-L**

# Chapter 2
# Ships

Quilt by the author, from the collection of Chuck and Ann Rupnow. Ships first appeared as the "Nautical Quilted Wall Hanging" in the January/February 1985 issue of *Needlecraft for Today*, and is included here by the kind permission of the editor.

## Remarks

This traditional *ship* or *sailboat* pattern is suitable for either a crib or youth bed. It is also appropriate as a wall quilt.

Ordinarily, Ships is constructed in a four-patch arrangement; however, this pattern has been designed to eliminate unnecessary cutting and piecing. Long intact panels have been placed between the rows of ships, and sections of the background have been consolidated from squares into larger rectangles. Sails and ship ends are constructed from tandem-pieced triangles.

Before you begin cutting the fabric, read through all the instructions *and* the Appendix, "How to Make Tandem-Pieced Triangles."

## For Starters

- Wash and press all fabrics before you begin.
- The quilt shown uses four fabrics.
- Each finished ship unit measures 12" X 9".
- The gold cross-lattices are 3" wide.
- The side borders are 3" wide, and the end borders (top and bottom) are 6" wide.
- The marking unit for the tandem-pieced triangles is 4¾".

- The finished paired triangle units measure 3" square.
- The seam width is ½".
- The finished size for Ships is 42" X 51".

## Supplies

### Quilt Top Fabric
Use 44"/45"–wide cotton or cotton/polyester blends.

| | |
|---|---|
| Gold solid | 2 yards (for background) |
| White print | ¾ yard (for sails) |
| Dark blue solid | ¾ yard (for ships) |
| Dark blue print | 1⅜ yards (for borders and binding) |

### Backing
Requires 1⅝ yards of bleached muslin.

### Batting
Choose either crib batting (45" X 60") or a 45" X 55" piece of bonded polyester.

### Other Supplies
- Regular sewing thread to match the fabrics
- A sewing machine
- A long straightedge
- A pencil
- One spool of white quilting thread

**Diagram 2-1. Gold Solid (G) Layout**

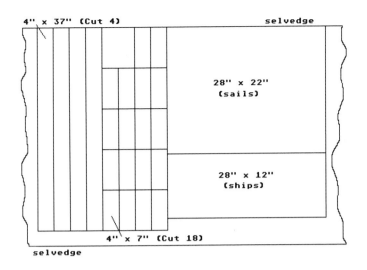

- Thread or safety pins for basting
- Soap chips or marking pencils
- Pins and quilting needles
- A large right triangle or T-square
- Scissors
- Template material for quilting designs
- A hoop or frame for quilting
- Optional: A rotary cutter and cutting mat

# Ready to Work

## Color Key
G   Gold solid
W   White print
B   Dark blue solid
P   Dark blue print

## Cutting
Begin with the gold (G) fabric and cut the following pieces, according to Diagram 2-1:

- 4 panels, 4" × 37" (½" seam allowances included)
- 18 rectangles, 4" × 7" (½" seam allowances included)
- 1 piece, 28" × 22" (for tandem piecing)
- 1 piece, 28" × 12" (for tandem piecing)

Next, cut a 22" × 28" piece from the white print (W) fabric, as shown in Diagram 2-2. This will be used for the tandem-pieced sails.

**Diagram 2-2. White Print (W) Layout**

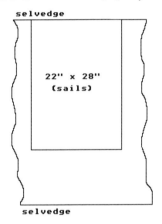

Next, cut the following ship pieces from the dark blue solid (B), as shown in Diagram 2-3:

- 9 rectangles, 4" × 7" (½" seam allowances included)
- 1 piece, 12" x 28" (for tandem piecing)

12

## Diagram 2-3. Dark Blue Solid (B) Layout

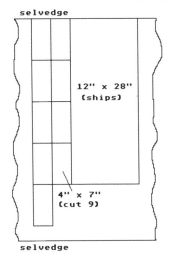

Finally, cut the following borders from the dark blue print (P), as shown in Diagram 2-4:

- 2 end borders, 43" × 7" (½" seam allowances included)
- 2 side borders, 40" × 4" (½" seam allowances included)

## Diagram 2-4. Dark Blue Print (P) Layout

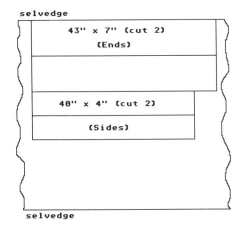

## Tandem Piecing

Begin with the 28" × 22" gold solid (G) piece. On the wrong side of the fabric (with the 22" edge horizontal, as shown in Diagram 2-5) mark a grid of 4¾" squares (4 squares across, 5 squares down) for a total of 20 squares, according to Diagram 2-5. Mark diagonal lines as shown.

## Diagram 2-5. Marking Grid for Gold Solid (G), 28" × 22"

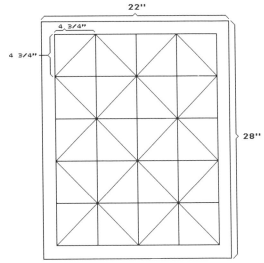

*Mark on **wrong** side of fabric with 22" edge horizontal.*

Pin this to the 22" × 28" piece of white print (W), with the right sides together. Stitch into tandem-pieced triangles using ½" seams, according to the directions in the Appendix, "How to Make Tandem-Pieced Triangles." Use the suggested continuous lines and directional arrows in Diagram 2-6 for the most efficient results.

## Diagram 2-6. Stitching Lines (½") for Gold (G) and White (W) Pieces

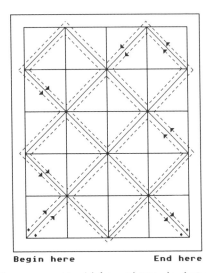

*Mark on **wrong** side of fabric with 22" edge horizontal.*

Cut, press, and trim each combination unit. You need 36 G/W pieced units, and you'll have a few extras.

Next, mark a grid of 4¾" squares on the 28" × 12" piece of gold fabric (with the 12" edge horizontal as shown in Diagram 2-7). Mark a total of ten squares (two across, five down), according to Diagram 2-7, and mark the diagonal lines as shown.

**Diagram 2-7. Marking Grid for Gold Solid (G)**

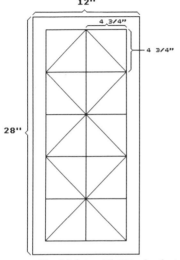

*Mark on **wrong** side of fabric, with 12" edge horizontal.*

With right sides of the fabric together, pin this to the 12" × 28" piece of dark blue solid (B), and stitch according to the suggested arrows in Diagram 2-8.

**Diagram 2-8. Stitching Lines (½") for Gold (G) and Dark Blue Solid (B) Pieces**

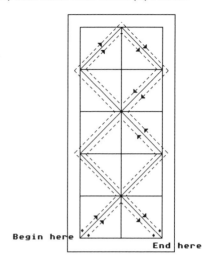

Cut, press, and trim each tandem-pieced unit as described above. You need 18 G/B units, and you'll have 2 extras.

# Putting It Together

### Assembly of Ships

The basic ship unit is a 12" × 9" rectangle, as shown in Diagram 2-9. Gather together two gold rectangles (4" × 7"), one dark blue solid rectangle (4" × 7"), four G/W tandem units, and two G/B tandem units, and arrange these according to Diagram 2-10. Follow the suggested order of piecing (seams 1–8) illustrated in Diagram 2-11. Make eight additional ships the same way.

**Diagram 2-9. Basic Ship Pattern**

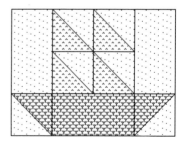

**Diagram 2-10. Arrangement of Gold (G), Dark Blue Solid (B), and White (W) Pieces in Ship Pattern**

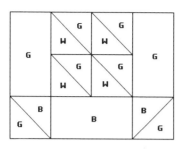

**Diagram 2-11. Ship Piecing Order**

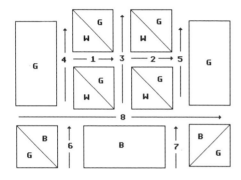

## Latticework and Borders

To assemble the quilt top, stitch the three ships of row 1 using ½" vertical seams, as shown in Diagram 2-12. Make two more rows like row 1.

**Diagram 2-12. Piecing Row 1 of Ships**

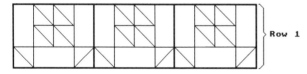

Add a 4" × 37" gold (G) panel at the top, between the rows, and at the bottom, according to Diagram 2-13. Add a 40" × 4" dark blue print (P) border lengthwise to each side. Finally, add a 43" × 7" border to the top and bottom to complete the quilt top.

**Diagram 2-13. Ships Layout**

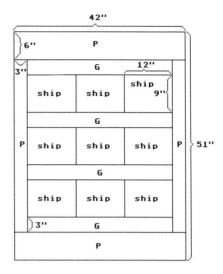

# The Finished Product

## Quilting

Place the 1⅝ yards of bleached muslin backing fabric right side down on a smooth surface. Smooth the batting over it, and place the pressed quilt top over the batting, right side up. Pin or baste the three layers together for quilting.

Quilt "in the ditch" around each ship and set of sails, and around the blocks, using white quilting thread. Mark and quilt lines ½" inside each ship and sail, and on each gold rectangle, according to Diagram 2-14.

**Diagram 2-14. Suggested Quilting for Ships**

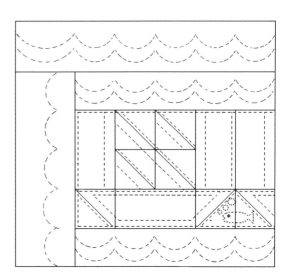

Make cardboard or plastic patterns of quilting designs 2-A (fish and bubbles) and 2-B (wave). Mark and quilt the wave pattern on the long gold panels and outer print borders, as shown in Diagram 2-14. Mark and quilt the fish and bubbles between the ships.

**Finishing**

Trim the batting to ½" larger than the quilt top to allow for filler in the binding. Trim the quilt back to match the top. Make 3"-wide bias strips from the remaining dark blue print (P) fabric. Piece the strips to a length of about 6 yards. For a finished binding of about ½", fold the binding wrong sides together and attach it to the quilt front, making sure the seam goes through all five layers. Turn the binding to the back of the quilt and whipstitch it in place.

**Design 2-A. Fish and Bubbles**

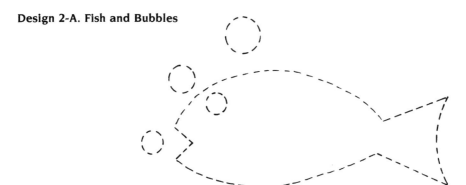

**Design 2-B. Wave**

# Chapter 3
# Nine-Patch Churn Dash

## Quilt by Marie Halmstad

## Remarks

Nine-Patch Churn Dash is a basic, equal-division pattern. It may seem familiar to you because it closely resembles several other traditional patterns, including Goose-in-the-Pond, Young Man's Fancy, Handy Andy, Sister's Choice, Churn Dash, and Duck and Ducklings. Don't be misled by the name *Nine-Patch Churn Dash*. The pattern is actually a basic five-patch design—it can be subdivided into five equal parts horizontally and vertically. The *nine-patch* name is applied because of the prominent nine-patch grouping of squares in the center. The *churn dash* name is applied because of the suggestion of larger dark triangles in the four corners.

Before you begin cutting the fabric, read through all the instructions *and* the Appendix, "How to Make Tandem-Pieced Triangles."

## For Starters

- Wash and press all fabrics before you begin.
- The finished blocks (a total of 20) each measure 17½" square.
- The latticework measures 3½" wide.

- The marking unit for the tandem-pieced triangles is 4⅜".
- The finished paired triangle units measure 3½" square.
- The corner squares measure 3½" wide.
- The seam width is ¼".
- The finished size for Nine-Patch Churn Dash is 87½" × 108½", appropriate for a standard double or queen-size bed.
- Four fabrics are required to complete the top.

## Supplies

**Quilt Top Fabric**
Use 44"/45"–wide cotton or cotton/polyester blends.

| | |
|---|---|
| Bold floral print | 2¾ yards |
| Fine floral print | 1½ yards |
| Dark solid (teal; includes binding) | 5 yards |
| Light solid (unbleached muslin) | 3½ yards |

**Backing**
Requires 6½ yards of unbleached muslin.

**Batting**
Use a 90" × 108" (queen size) piece of bonded polyester.

## Other Supplies

- Regular sewing thread to match the fabrics
- A sewing machine
- A long straightedge
- A pencil
- Two spools of natural-color quilting thread
- Thread or safety pins for basting
- Soap chips or marking pencils
- Pins and quilting needles
- A large right triangle or T-square
- Scissors
- A hoop or frame for quilting
- Optional: A rotary cutter and cutting mat

# Ready to Work

## Color Key

B   Bold print
F   Fine print
T   Teal (dark solid)
M   Unbleached muslin (light solid)

## Cutting

Begin with the bold print (B) and cut the following pieces, according to Diagram 3-1:

- 20 squares, each 4" × 4" (¼" seam allowances included)

Set aside the remaining fabric for tandem piecing.

**Diagram 3-1. Layout for Bold Print (B)**

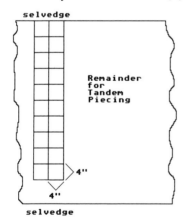

Cut the following pieces from the fine print (F), according to Diagram 3-2:

- 110 squares, each 4" × 4" (¼" seam allowances included)

**Diagram 3-2. Layout for Fine Print (F)**

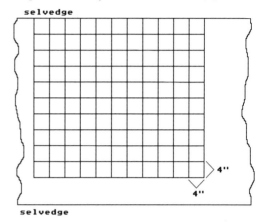

Cut the following from the teal fabric (T), according to Diagram 3-3:

- 80 squares, each 4" × 4" (¼" seam allowances included)
- 49 lattices, each 18" × 4" (¼" seam allowances included)

Set aside the remaining fabric for binding.

Cut the following from the unbleached muslin (M), according to Diagram 3-4:

- 80 squares, each 4" × 4" (¼" seam allowances included)

Set aside the remaining fabric for tandem piecing.

## Tandem Piecing

Begin with the remaining unbleached muslin (M) fabric. Cut two 1-yard pieces for easy handling. On the wrong side of a 1-yard piece, mark a grid of 4⅜"-inch squares (7 squares across, 9 squares down) for a total of 63 squares, according to Diagram 3-5, and mark the diagonal lines as shown. Similarly mark the other 1-yard piece of muslin.

**Diagram 3-3. Layout for Teal (T)**

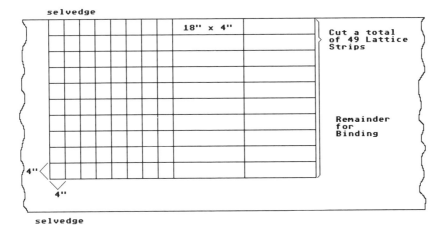

selvedge

18" x 4"

Cut a total
of 49 Lattice
Strips

Remainder
for
Binding

4"

4"

selvedge

**Diagram 3-4. Layout for Unbleached Muslin (M)**

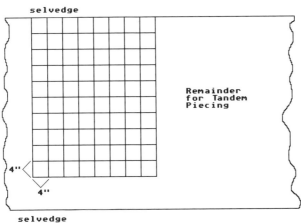

selvedge

Remainder
for Tandem
Piecing

4"

4"

selvedge

**Diagram 3-5. Marking Grid for Unbleached Muslin (M)**

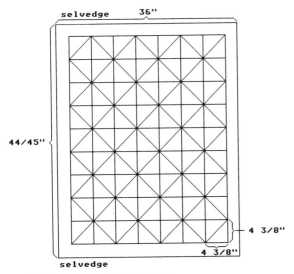

selvedge   36"

44/45"

4 3/8"

4 3/8"

selvedge

*Mark on **wrong** side of the fabric.*

Next, cut two 1-yard pieces from the remaining bold print (B) fabric. Pin each piece to a marked muslin piece, with the right sides together. Stitch into tandem-pieced triangles using ¼" seams, according to the directions in the Appendix, "How to Make Tandem-Pieced Triangles." Use the suggested continuous lines and directional arrows illustrated in Diagram 3-6 for the most efficient results.

## Diagram 3-6. Stitching Lines (¼")

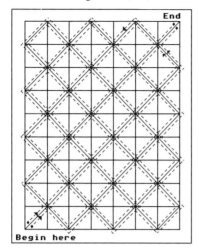

Cut, press, and trim each combination unit. You should have 240 B/M pieced units, with a few left over.

# Putting It Together

## Assembly of Nine-Patch Churn Dash Blocks

Each block consists of 13 squares (1 bold print, 4 fine print, 4 teal, and 4 muslin) and 12 tandem triangle units. Gather the necessary units to complete the block as shown in Diagram 3-7. Lay the units right sides up. Piece row 1 together using vertical seams (¼"), according to Diagram 3-8. Piece rows 2, 3, 4, and 5 likewise.

## Diagram 3-7. Assembly of a Nine-Patch Churn Dash Block

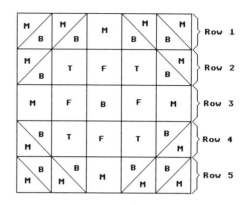

## Diagram 3-8. Piecing Row 1 of Nine-Patch Churn Dash Block

Press the seams of rows 1, 3, and 5 to one side. Press the seams of rows 2 and 4 in the opposite direction. Join the five rows in horizontal seams, being careful to "butterfly" the seams at the intersections in order to minimize bulk. This will happen naturally if the rows are pressed as directed above. Press all horizontal seams in one direction. The completed block is shown in Diagram 3-9.

Assemble the remaining 19 blocks in a similar fashion.

## Diagram 3-9. Completed Nine-Patch Churn Dash Block

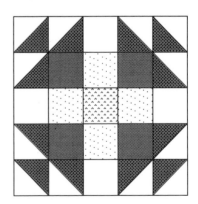

Four-Patch Sampler

Dorothy's Dilemma

Holiday Quick Quilt

Bow Tie Wall Quilt

Ships

Detail of Dorothy's Dilemma Showing Quilt Designs 5-A and 5-B on Chevron and Diamond Shapes

Detail of Holiday Quick Quilt Showing Border

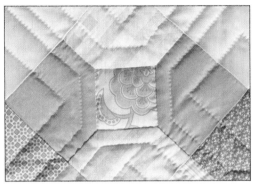

Detail of Bow Tie Wall Quilt

Detail of Ships

Detail of Nine-Patch Churn Dash Showing Design in Block and Cable Quilting on Lattices

Detail of Pieced Star Wall Quilt Showing Border and Quilting Designs

Nine-Patch Churn Dash

Pieced Star Wall Quilt

Sweet Dreams Crib Quilt

Computer Symmetry

Little Red Schoolhouse

## Latticework

Gather four Nine-Patch Churn Dash blocks and five lattice strips (T). Assemble these into a row, as in Diagram 3-10. Make five of these rows.

**Diagram 3-10. Pieced Lattice Strips and Blocks**

Lattice (T)

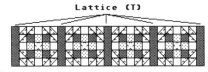

*Make five of these rows.*

Next, gather four lattice strips (T) and five corner squares (F); assemble into a row, as in Diagram 3-11. Make six of these rows.

**Diagram 3-11. Pieced Lattice Strips and Corner Squares**

*Make six of these rows.*

Stitch the lattice-and-corner-square panels and the lattice-and-block panels together horizontally to complete the quilt top, using Diagram 3-12 as your guide.

**Diagram 3-12. Nine-Patch Churn Dash Layout**

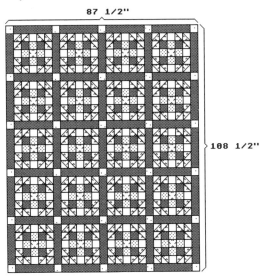

# The Finished Product

## Quilting

Cut the 6½ yards of muslin backing into two 3¼-yard lengths. Leave one length intact. Split the other into two 22" panels and stitch to each side of the intact panel. Press the seams to the outside.

Place the backing right side down, and smooth the batting over it. Place the pressed quilt top over the batting, right side up. Be sure the batting extends beyond the edges of the quilt top. Pin or baste the three layers together for quilting.

With a straightedge and soap chip or marking pencil, mark quilting lines ¼" from the seams on all squares and triangles, according to Diagram 3-13. Mark the cable quilting design, according to Diagram 3-14, on each lattice strip. Quilt along all marked lines using the natural-color quilting thread.

**Diagram 3-13. Suggested Quilting for Nine-Patch Churn Dash**

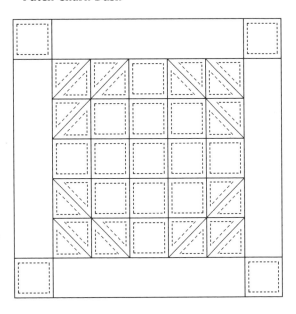

**Diagram 3-14. Cable Quilting
Design for Lattices**

3 1/2"

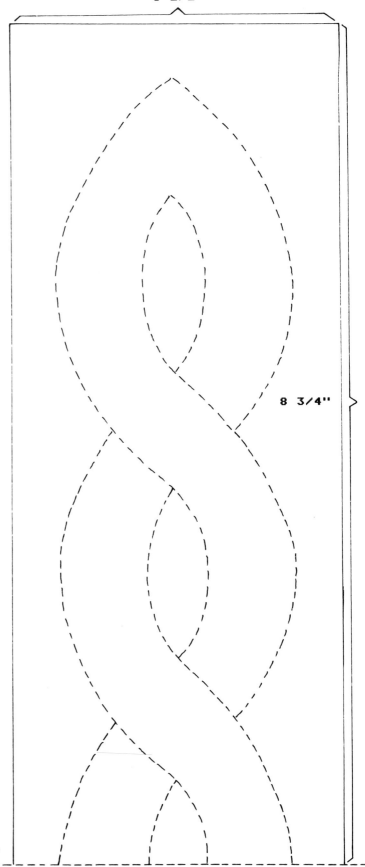

8 3/4"

**Lattice Center**

## Finishing

Trim the batting to ½" larger than the quilt top to allow for filler in the binding. Trim the quilt backing to match the top. Make 3"-wide continuous bias binding from the remaining teal (T) fabric. (Instructions for making continuous binding are included in the book *Award-Winning Quilts and How to Make Them*.)

For a finished binding of about ½", fold the binding, wrong sides together, and attach it to the quilt front, making sure the seam goes through all five layers. Turn the binding to the back of the quilt and whipstitch it in place.

# Chapter 4
# Pieced Star Wall Quilt

Quilt by Marky Kuba

## Remarks

This four-patch star pattern is known by several names, among them Pieced Star, Pierced Star, Barbara Frietchie Star, and Star Puzzle. In Marky's quilt, the star is set in a format that creates a secondary design at the intersections where four blocks come together. This secondary design resembles the traditional Shoo-Fly or Churn Dash pattern shown in Diagram 4-16.

Before you begin cutting the fabric, read through all the instructions *and* the Appendix, "How to Make Tandem-Pieced Triangles."

## For Starters

- Wash and press all fabrics before you begin.
- The quilt shown uses four fabrics.
- The paired triangle units, measuring 2" finished, are made from 2⅞" marked squares.
- Latticework measures 1" wide.
- The outer border measures 3" wide.
- Each of the 12 finished blocks measures 8" square.
- The seam width is ¼".
- The finished size for the Pieced Star Wall Quilt is 34" × 43".

## Supplies

### Quilt Top Fabric
Use 44"/45"–wide cotton or cotton/polyester blends.

| | |
|---|---|
| Black print | 1¼ yards (for stars and binding) |
| Rust print | 1¼ yards (for stars and border) |
| Gold print | ⅜ yard (for stars) |
| Unbleached muslin | 1⅝ yards (for stars and latticework) |

### Backing
Use 1¾ yards of unbleached muslin.

### Batting
Choose either crib batting (45" × 60") or a 36" × 48" piece of bonded polyester.

### Other Supplies
- Regular sewing thread to match the fabrics
- A sewing machine
- A long straightedge
- A pencil
- One spool of natural-color quilting thread
- Thread or safety pins for basting
- Soap chips or marking pencils
- Pins and quilting needles

- A large right triangle or T-square
- Scissors
- A hoop or frame for quilting
- Optional: A rotary cutter and cutting mat

# Ready to Work

## Color Key
B   Black print
R   Rust print
G   Gold print
M   Unbleached muslin

## Cutting
Begin with the black print (B) and cut the following pieces, according to Diagram 4-1:

- 1 piece, 10" × 27" (for tandem piecing)
- 1 piece, 9" × 1½" (for lattice corners)

Save the remaining black print fabric for binding.

**Diagram 4-1. Layout for Black Print (B)**

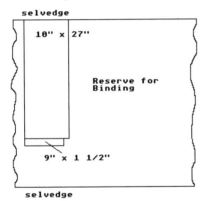

Cut the following pieces from the rust print (R), according to Diagram 4-2:

- 1 piece, 27" × 20" (for tandem piecing)
- 2 side borders, 37½" × 3½" (seam allowances included)
- 2 end borders, 34½" × 3½" (seam allowances included)

**Diagram 4-2. Layout for Rust Print (R)**

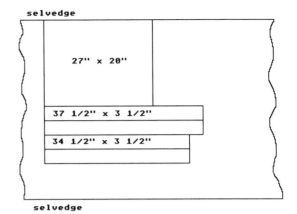

Cut a 10" × 27" piece from the gold print (G), according to Diagram 4-3.

**Diagram 4-3. Layout for Gold Print (G)**

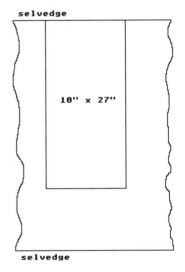

Cut the following pieces from the 1⅝-yard piece of unbleached muslin (M), according to Diagram 4-4:

For tandem piecing,
- 1 piece, 27" × 20"
- 2 pieces, 27" × 10"

For lattices (seam allowances included),
- 1 piece, 8½" × 9"
- 11 pieces, 8½" × 1½"
- 2 sides, 1½" × 35½"
- 2 ends, 1½" × 28½"

**Diagram 4-4. Layout for Unbleached Muslin (M)**

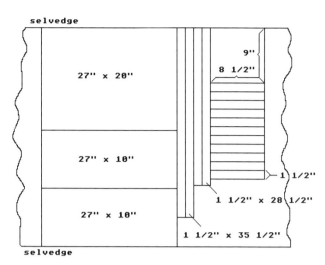

selvedge

27" x 20"

9"

8 1/2"

27" x 10"

1 1/2"

1 1/2" x 28 1/2"

27" x 10"

1 1/2" x 35 1/2"

selvedge

### Tandem Piecing

Begin with the 27" × 20" piece of unbleached muslin (M). On the wrong side of the fabric, mark a grid of 2⅞" squares (8 squares across, 6 squares down) for a total of 48 squares, according to Diagram 4-5, and mark the diagonal lines as shown. Pin this to the 27" × 20" piece of rust print (R), with the right sides together, and stitch into tandem-pieced triangles using ¼" seams, according to the directions in the Appendix, "How to Make Tandem-Pieced Triangles."

Use the suggested continuous stitching lines and directional arrows illustrated in Diagram 4-6 for the most efficient results. Cut, press, and trim each combination unit. You should have 96 M/R pieced units.

**Diagram 4-6. Stitching Lines (¼")**

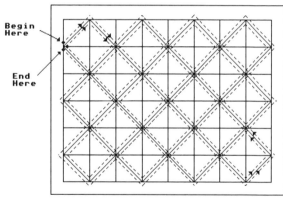

Begin Here

End Here

**Diagram 4-5. Marking Grid for Unbleached Muslin (M)**

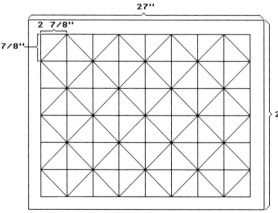

27"

2 7/8"

7/8"

20"

*Mark on **wrong** side of the fabric.*

On each of the two 27" × 10" pieces of unbleached muslin (M), mark a grid of 2⅞" squares (8 squares across and 3 squares down, for a total of 24 squares) on the wrong side of the fabric, according to Diagram 4-7. Mark the diagonal lines as shown. With the right sides together, pin one piece of muslin to a 10" × 27" piece of black print (B), with the 27" edges horizontal. Pin the other piece of unbleached muslin to the

10" × 27" piece of gold print (G) with the 27" edges horizontal. Stitch according to the suggested directional arrows shown in Diagram 4-7. Cut, press, and trim into tandem-pieced units, as previously described. You should have 48 B/M pieced units and 48 G/M pieced units.

**Diagram 4-7. Marking Grid and Stitching Lines (¼")**

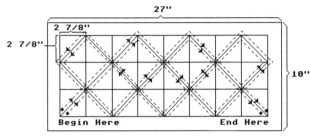

*Mark on **wrong** side of the fabric.*

# Putting It Together

## Assembly of Stars

Each star consists of 16 paired-triangle square units. Gather four M/B units, four M/G units, and eight M/R units. Lay the units, right sides up, according to Diagram 4-8. Piece row 1 together using short vertical ¼" seams, according to Diagram 4-9. Similarly piece rows 2, 3, and 4.

**Diagram 4-8. Pieced Star Pattern**

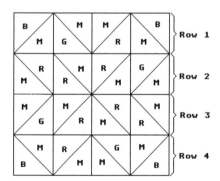

**Diagram 4-9. Piecing Row 1 of Star Pattern**

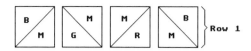

Press the seams of rows 1 and 3 to one side, and press the seams of rows 2 and 4 in the opposite direction. Join the four rows using horizontal seams, being careful to "butterfly" the seams at the intersections in order to minimize bulk. This will happen naturally if the rows are pressed as directed above. Press all horizontal seams to one side. The completed block is shown in Diagram 4-10. Assemble the remaining 11 blocks in a similar fashion.

**Diagram 4-10. Completed Pieced Star Block**

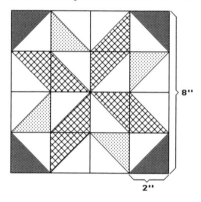

## Latticework

The latticework is 1" wide when finished. With right sides together, piece the 1½" × 9" piece of black print (B) and the 8½" × 9" piece of unbleached muslin (M) using a ¼" seam (with the 9" edges together), according to Diagram 4-11.

**Diagram 4-11. Pieced Latticework Panel Before Cutting**

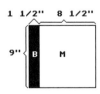

38

Mark and cut the assembled panel into six 1½"-wide strips, according to Diagram 4-12. You can do this easily with the rotary cutter, ruler, and mat.

**Diagram 4-12. Cutting Lines for Latticework Panel**

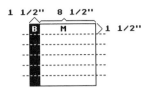

Stitch three pieced lattice strips together, as shown in Diagram 4-13, and add a plain 1½" × 8½" muslin (M) strip at the bottom. Make two of these latticework columns.

**Diagram 4-13. Pieced Latticework Column**

Assemble a column of four pieced stars and three 1½" × 8½" muslin strips, according to Diagram 4-14. Make three of these columns.

**Diagram 4-14. Pieced Star Column**

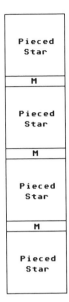

Stitch the star columns and the latticework columns together vertically to complete the quilt center, using Diagram 4-15 as your guide. Secondary designs resembling the Shoo-Fly or Churn Dash pattern shown in Diagram 4-16 will appear at the intersections. Next, add the long muslin strips— first to the sides and then to the ends.

**Diagram 4-15. Layout Showing Pieced Star Blocks, Latticework, and Borders**

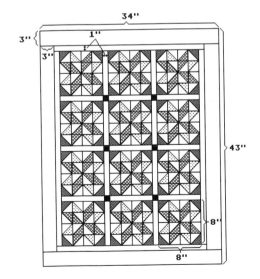

**Diagram 4-16. Shoo-Fly or Churn Dash Design**

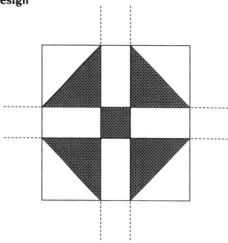

**Diagram 4-17. Suggested Quilting for Pieced Star Wall Quilt**

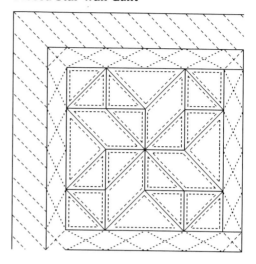

## Borders

Add the 3½" rust print (R) borders (sides first, then ends) as shown in Diagram 4-15 to complete the quilt top.

# The Finished Product

## Quilting

Place the 1¾-yard muslin backing fabric right side down, smooth the batting over it, and place the pressed quilt top over the batting, right side up. Pin or baste the three layers together for quilting.

Mark quilting lines (¼" from all seam lines) with a straightedge and soap chip or marking pencil, according to Diagram 4-17, and quilt along all marked lines using the natural-color quilting thread.

## Finishing

Trim the batting to ½" larger than the quilt top to allow for filler in the binding, and trim the quilt backing to match the top. Make 3"-wide bias strips from the remaining black print (B) fabric, and piece the strips to a length of about 5 yards. For a finished binding of about ½", fold the binding wrong sides together and attach it to the quilt front, making sure the seam goes through all five layers. Turn the binding to the back of the quilt and whipstitch it in place.

# Chapter 5
# Dorothy's Dilemma

## Quilt by Dorothy Gilbertson

## Remarks

Dorothy's Dilemma is an original design based on the traditional double four-patch pattern (16 units in each block pattern). The light/dark combinations and pieced blocks come together to form secondary chevron-like designs. Other shapes formed or suggested are diamonds, arrows, the letter C (as in C-clamp), and a collarlike shape.

Only two fabrics (a light and a dark) are needed, so fabric selection should be an easy task. Dorothy's Dilemma is also an easy quilt to assemble, although some thought must be given to the placement of units and the additional side panels. Dorothy's Dilemma is a *directional* pattern and not entirely symmetrical, so blocks must be carefully assembled. The diagrams will be very helpful in this respect, so follow them carefully.

Curved hand-quilting designs complement and help soften the sharper geometric lines of the piecing and are easy to mark and quilt.

Before you begin cutting fabric, read through all the instructions *and* the Appendix, "How to Make Tandem-Pieced Triangles."

## For Starters

- Wash and press all fabrics before you begin.
- The quilt shown uses only two fabrics.
- The paired triangle units, measuring 4¼", are made from marked 6" squares.
- The quilt is assembled from 20 blocks that each measure 17" square.
- Pieced panels are added to each side of the quilt to complete the design.
- Borders are 4" wide.
- All seams are ½".
- The finished size for Dorothy's Dilemma is 85½" × 94", adequate for a double bed.

## Supplies

### Quilt Top Fabric
Use 44"/45"-wide cotton or cotton/polyester blends.

Light print 6 yards (for blocks)
Dark print 9 yards (for blocks, borders, and binding)

### Backing
Use 6 yards of unbleached muslin.

### Batting
Use a 90" × 108" (queen size) piece of bonded polyester.

## Other Supplies
- Regular sewing thread to match the fabrics
- A sewing machine
- A long straightedge
- A pencil
- Two spools of natural-color quilting thread
- Thread or safety pins for basting
- Soap chips or marking pencils
- Pins and quilting needles
- Template material for making quilt stencils
- A large right triangle or T-square
- Scissors
- A hoop or frame for quilting
- Optional: A rotary cutter and cutting mat

# Ready to Work

## Color Key
L   Light print
D   Dark solid

## Cutting
Begin with the light print (L). Cut five pieces, each 1 yard long (36" × 45"), and cut one piece 8" long (8" × 45"). These will be used for tandem piecing.

Next, from the dark solid (D), cut five pieces, each 1 yard long (36" × 45"), and cut one piece 8" long (8" × 45"). From the remaining dark fabric, cut the following borders:

- 2 side borders, 5" x 94" (½" seam allowances included)
- 2 end borders, 5" × 85½" (½" seam allowances included)

Set the remaining dark solid aside for binding.

## Tandem Piecing
Begin with a 36" piece of light print (L). On the wrong side of the fabric mark a grid of 6" squares (5 squares across, 7 squares down) for a total of 35 squares, according to Diagram 5-1, and mark diagonal lines as shown.

**Diagram 5-1. Marking Grid for 36" Piece of Light Print (L)**

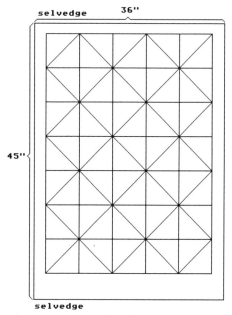

*Mark on **wrong** side of the fabric.*

Pin this piece to a 36" piece of dark solid (D), right sides together, and using ½" seams, stitch into tandem-pieced triangles according to the directions in the Appendix, "How to Make Tandem-Pieced Triangles." Use the suggested continuous stitching lines and directional arrows shown in Diagram 5-2 for the best results.

**Diagram 5-2. Stitching Lines (½")**

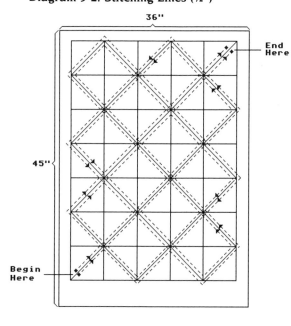

Cut into squares and triangles, press the seams toward the dark fabric, and trim each combination unit. You should have 70 L/D pieced units like the one shown in Diagram 5-3.

### Diagram 5-3. L/D Pieced Unit for Dorothy's Dilemma

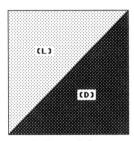

(L)

(D)

*You will need a total of 360 of these units.*

Mark the other four 36" pieces of light print (L) in a similar way; then stitch, cut, press, and trim the additional units. You'll have 350 L/D pieced units.

On the 8" × 45" piece of light print, mark seven 6" squares as shown in Diagram 5-4. Pin this piece to the 8" × 45" piece of dark solid, right sides together, and stitch according to the suggested arrows in Diagram 5-4. Cut, press, and trim each unit as described before. You'll have 14 L/D pieced units from this fabric.

### Diagram 5-4. Marking Grid and Stitching Lines (½") for 8" Piece of Light Print

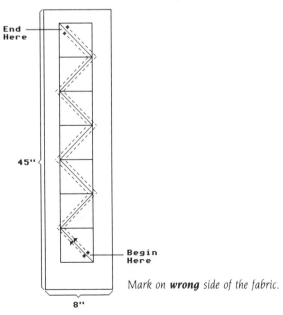

End Here

45"

Begin Here

*Mark on **wrong** side of the fabric.*

8"

You need a combined total of 360 of these combination units. You'll have 4 extras.

# Putting It Together

## Assembly of Blocks

Each block consists of 16 tandem-pieced units. Gather 16 units and lay them, right sides up, according to Diagram 5-5. Piece row 1 together using short vertical ½" seams, according to Diagram 5-6. Similarly piece rows 2, 3, and 4.

### Diagram 5-5. Piecing Arrangement for a Block of Dorothy's Dilemma

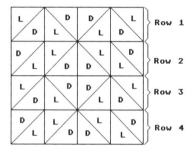

Row 1
Row 2
Row 3
Row 4

### Diagram 5-6. Piecing Row 1 of a Block

Row 1

Press the seams of rows 1 and 3 to one side, and press the seams of rows 2 and 4 in the opposite direction. Join the four rows using horizontal seams, being careful to "butterfly" the seams at the intersections in order to minimize bulk—this will occur naturally if the rows are pressed as directed. Press all horizontal seams to one side.

The completed block is shown in Diagram 5-7. Assemble the remaining 19 blocks in a similar fashion.

**Diagram 5-7. Completed Block of Dorothy's Dilemma**

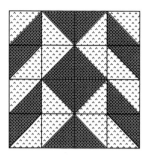

To assemble the quilt top, pin together the four blocks comprising the top row (in the same way you pieced row 1 for a block, as shown in Diagram 5-6). Stitch the blocks together using ½" vertical seams, and press the seams to one side. Similarly join the blocks throughout the quilt top, and stitch the five rows using long horizontal seams.

## Assembly of Side Panels

In order to complete the design in Dorothy's Dilemma, a long pieced panel is added to each side (the panels are different from each other). The *left* panel is shown in Diagram 5-8, and is easiest to piece in small four-block units as shown in Diagram 5-9. To complete the panel, stitch together 5 four-block units. The finished panel is 20 units long.

**Diagram 5-8. Left Panel of 20 L/D Units**

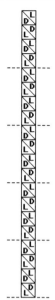

**Diagram 5-9. Left Panel Four-Block Unit**

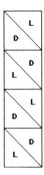

*Make five of these.*

The *right* panel is shown in Diagram 5-10, and is easiest to piece in four-block units as shown in Diagram 5-11. To complete the panel, stitch 5 four-block units together.

Add the left and right panels to the assembled 20-block quilt top.

**Diagram 5-10. Right Panel of 20 L/D Units**

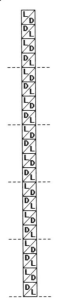

**Diagram 5-11. Right Panel Four-Block Unit**

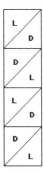

*Make five of these.*

### Borders

Add the dark solid (D) borders to the sides and ends, mitering all corners. This completes the quilt top as shown in Diagram 5-12.

**Diagram 5-12. Dorothy's Dilemma Layout**

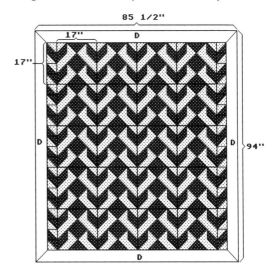

# The Finished Product

### Quilting

Cut the 6 yards of unbleached muslin backing fabric into two 3-yard lengths, leaving one length intact. Split the other length into two 22" panels and stitch to each side of the intact piece. Press the seams to the outside.

Place the backing right side down, and smooth the batting over it. Place the pressed quilt top over the batting, right side up, and pin or baste the three layers together for quilting.

With a straightedge and soap chip or marking pencil, mark quilting lines on the large light print shapes ½" from the seam lines, according to Diagram 5-13. Quilt along these lines using the natural-color quilting thread, and quilt ''in the ditch'' (close to the seam) around the light print shapes.

**Diagram 5-13. Suggested Quilting for Dorothy's Dilemma**

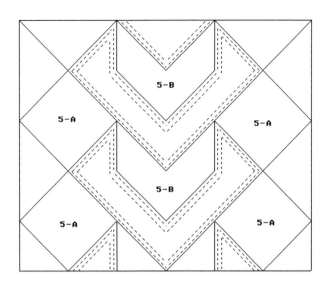

Make templates of the four curved quilt designs, 5-A, 5-B, 5-C, and 5-D. Then mark and quilt these designs on the dark solid areas and borders as follows:

• Design 5-A on the diamond shapes

• Design 5-B on the chevron shapes
• Design 5-C on the borders
• Design 5-D on the corners

Quilt "in the ditch" between the dark borders and the center pieced area.

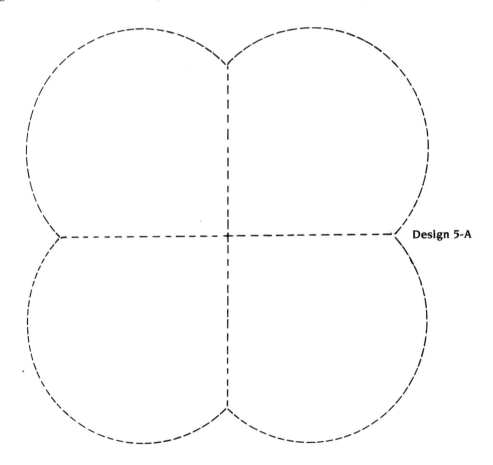

Design 5-A

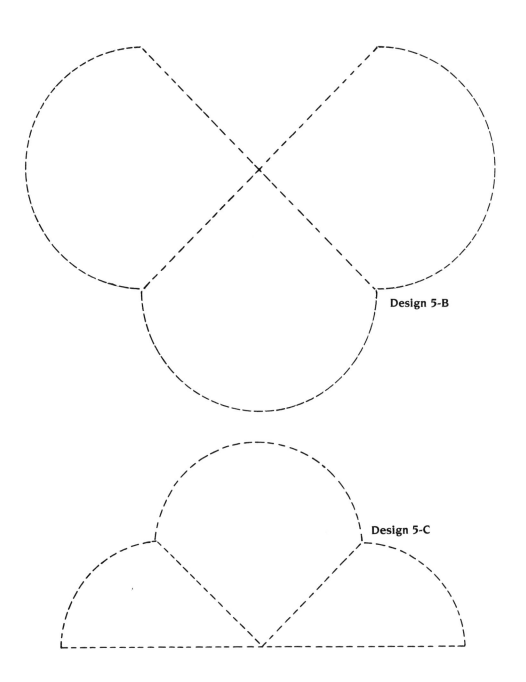

**Design 5-B**

**Design 5-C**

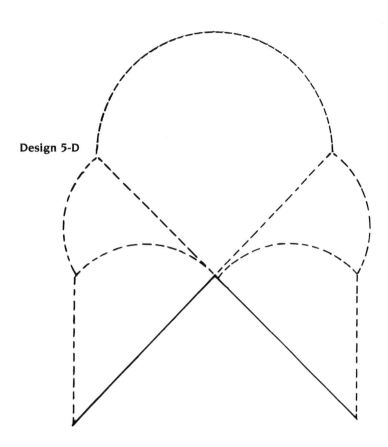

**Design 5-D**

## Finishing

Trim the batting to ¾" larger than the quilt top to allow for filler in the binding, and trim the backing to match the top.

Make 3½"-wide continuous bias binding from the remaining dark solid (D) fabric—you'll need a piece of fabric (piece it into a square, if necessary) about 40" square.

For a finished binding about ¾" wide, fold the binding wrong sides together and attach it to the quilt front, making sure the seam goes through all five layers. Turn the binding to the back of the quilt and whipstitch it in place.

# Part II
# Other
# Quick Quilts

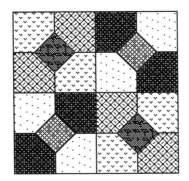

# Chapter 6
# Sweet Dreams Crib Quilt

Quilt by the author, from the collection of
Kiko and Kristen Lugo-Mendez, Märsta, Sweden.

## Remarks

Sweet Dreams is a pattern appropriate for beginning, as well as experienced, quilters. The cutting and piecing methods have been streamlined for maximum efficiency, and the use of a plaid fabric gives the illusion of intricate piecing. The fabric used here is a lightweight shirting material.

Sweet Dreams can easily be pieced in a day; a little more time is required for the hand-quilting. The gentle curves of the quilted hearts give relief from the sharper geometric lines of the squares and plaids, and the result is a lovely crib quilt that any family with a baby would be grateful to receive.

## For Starters

- Wash and press all fabrics before you begin.
- The quilt shown uses two fabrics: a pastel woven plaid and a coordinating light solid.
- The quilt uses 4" squares.
- Seam width is ¼".
- The finished size for Sweet Dreams is 38" X 48½".

## Supplies

### Quilt Top Fabric
Use 44"/45"–wide cotton or cotton/polyester blends.

| | |
|---|---|
| Light solid (aqua) | 1½ yards |
| Pastel plaid | 1½ yards |

### Binding
Use ¾ yard of medium light solid (aqua).

### Backing
Requires 1½ yards of bleached muslin.

### Batting
Choose either crib batting (45" X 60") or a 40" X 50"piece of bonded polyester.

### Other Supplies
- Regular sewing thread to match the fabrics
- A sewing machine
- A long straightedge
- A pencil
- One spool of white quilting thread
- Thread or safety pins for basting

- Soap chips or marking pencils
- Pins and quilting needles
- A large right triangle or T-square
- Scissors
- Template material for quilting designs
- A hoop or frame for quilting
- Optional: A rotary cutter and cutting mat

# Ready to Work

## Color Key
S  Light solid
P  Pastel plaid

## Cutting
The light solid and plaid fabrics for this quilt can both be cut most efficiently by folding the fabric in crosswise folds and then using a rotary cutter and straightedge, or a pair of good-quality scissors, to cut through the multiple thicknesses in long strips.

*Light solid fabric.* For the light solid (S) fabric, follow the cutting layout given in Diagram 6-1 to cut the borders and panels to be used for strip piecing.

**Diagram 6-1. Cutting Layout for Light Solid (S) Fabric**

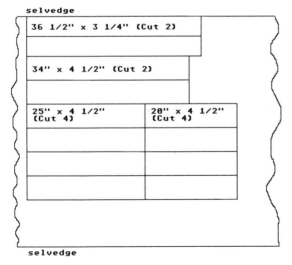

First, cut the two 3¼" strips for the side borders and trim these to 36½"; then cut two 4½" strips for the end borders and trim these to 34". Set these aside for now.

Cut four 4½" strips (each will be more than 50" long), and trim these to make four 25" panels and four 20" panels.

**Diagram 6-2. Cutting Layout for Plaid (P) Fabric**

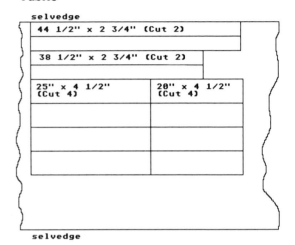

*Plaid fabric.* Cut the plaid fabric (P) according to Diagram 6-2, using the same folding and cutting technique used for the solid fabric.

First, cut the four 2¾" border strips; trim two to 44½", and the remaining two to 38½". Set these aside for now.

Cut the four 4½" strips (each will be more than 50" long), and trim these to make four 25" panels and four 20" panels.

# Putting It Together

## Strip Piecing
The central design for the Sweet Dreams crib quilt is based on two assembled strip panels designated *Unit* A and *Unit* B. These are shown in Diagrams 6-3 and 6-4.

**Diagram 6-3. Unit A Assembled 25" Strip Panel**

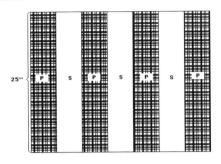

**Diagram 6-4. Unit B Assembled 20" Strip Panel**

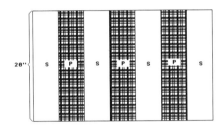

Begin with Unit A. Gather seven 25" strips (four plaid strips, three solid strips) and assemble these using ¼" seams, according to Diagram 6-3. Press all seams toward the plaid fabric.

To assemble Unit B, use seven 20" strips (four solid strips, three plaid strips), and stitch these in ¼" seams, according to Diagram 6-4. Press all seams toward the plaid fabric. You will have two leftover strips.

Cut the assembled panels into 4½" strips, as shown in Diagrams 6-5 and 6-6. Cut five strips from Unit A and four from Unit B.

**Diagram 6-5. Unit A Cutting Lines**

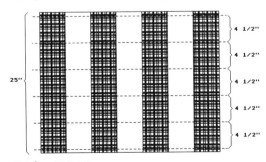

*Cut five 4½" strips.*

**Diagram 6-6. Unit B Cutting Lines**

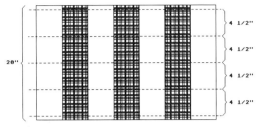

*Cut four 4½" strips.*

To assemble the quilt center, begin with a strip from Unit A (P-S-P-S-P-S-P). This will be row 1, as shown in Diagram 6-7, and row 2 will be a strip from Unit B (S-P-S-P-S-P-S). Alternate strips to complete the nine rows in a checkerboard fashion, and then join the rows using ¼" horizontal seams, being careful to "butterfly" the seams at each intersection. This should occur naturally if the panels are pressed as suggested. Press all cross-seams to one side.

**Diagram 6-7. Checkerboard Center of Sweet Dreams Crib Quilt**

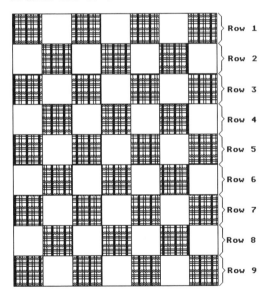

53

## Borders

Add the 2¾" solid (S) side borders according to Diagram 6-8; then add the 4" solid (S) end borders. Next, add the 2¼" plaid (P) side borders, and to complete the top, add the 2¼" plaid (P) end borders.

**Diagram 6-8. Layout Showing Placement of Borders**

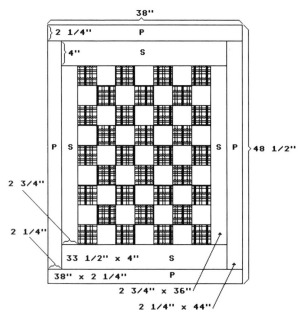

**Diagram 6-9. Suggested Quilting for Sweet Dreams Crib Quilt**

# The Finished Product

## Quilting

Place the 1½ yards of bleached muslin backing fabric right side down and smooth the batting over it. Place the pressed quilt top over the batting, right side up, and pin or baste the three layers together for quilting.

Make cardboard or plastic patterns of the two quilting designs, 6-A (heart) and 6-B (elongated heart motif). Mark and quilt a heart on each light solid square using white quilting thread, as suggested in Diagram 6-9. Outline the quilt on the inside of each solid square, about ¼" from the edge. Mark and quilt the elongated heart motif on the solid borders, placing three motifs on each side border and three on each end border.

Quilt "in the ditch" around each square and between the borders. Outline the quilt on the inside of each plaid square, about ¼" from the edge. Quilt a gridwork of two horizontal lines and two vertical lines along selected color lines on each plaid square and on the plaid border.

## Finishing

Trim the batting to ½" larger than the quilt top to allow for filler in the binding, and trim the quilt backing to match the top. Make 3"-wide bias strips from the ¾-yard medium light binding fabric, and piece the strips to a length of about 6 yards. For a finished binding of about ½", fold the binding wrong sides together and attach it to the quilt front, making sure the seam goes through all five layers. Turn the binding to the back of the quilt and whipstitch it in place.

**Design 6-A. Heart Motif**

**Design 6-B. Elongated Heart Motif**

# Chapter 7
# Holiday Quick Quilt

Quilt by the author

## Remarks

The Holiday Quick Quilt is pieced from carefully selected plaid squares set against a deep burgundy background, and is bordered by panels of deep forest green and contrasting corner squares.

The quilt top requires only three templates, and the steps for unit piecing are both quick and easy. The top is completed with a combination of geometric and curved quilting lines that flow from the center into the borders, and it is bound alternately with burgundy and green for optimum border contrast.

## For Starters

- Wash and press all fabrics before you begin.
- The quilt shown requires three fabrics: burgundy, forest green, and a multicolor plaid.
- Plaid squares are cut from two different design areas on the plaid fabric.
- The green borders are 5½" wide, and the four corners measure 5½" square.
- Seam width is ¼".
- The finished size for the Holiday Quick Quilt is 28" X 33".

## Supplies

### Quilt Top Fabric
Use 44"/45"–wide cotton or cotton/polyester blends.

| | |
|---|---|
| Burgundy | ¾ yard |
| Forest green | ½ yard |
| Plaid | ½ yard (Use more if the plaid is very wide or if you prefer uniformly cut squares, as pictured.) |

### Backing
Requires 1 yard of unbleached muslin.

### Batting
Choose either crib batting (45" X 60") or a 30" X 35" piece of bonded polyester.

### Other Supplies
- Regular sewing thread to match the fabrics
- A sewing machine
- A long straightedge
- A pencil
- One spool of natural-color quilting thread
- Thread or safety pins for basting
- Soap chips or marking pencils
- Pins and quilting needles
- Scissors

- Cardboard or plastic for templates
- A hoop or frame for quilting

# Ready to Work

### Color Key

B Burgundy
G Forest green
PA Plaid (design area A)
PB Plaid (design area B)

### Cutting

First, make plastic or cardboard templates for the square and two triangles (Templates 7-1, 7-2, and 7-3).

Note: ¼" seam allowances must be added. Be certain to indicate the grain-line arrow on each template.

Begin with the burgundy fabric (B) and cut the following pieces:

- 10 large triangles (Template 7-1)
- 20 small triangles (Template 7-2)
- 6 squares (Template 7-3)
- 2 strips, 1½" × 25" (for binding)
- 2 strips, 1½" × 20" (for binding)

Next, cut the following pieces from the forest green (G):

- 2 side borders, 6" × 22½" (¼" seam allowances included)
- 2 end borders, 6" × 17" (¼" seam allowances included)
- 4 strips, 1½" × 15" (for binding)

Last, cut the squares from the plaid fabric (P). Examine the plaid fabric for interesting design areas, and select two areas that contrast somewhat with each other. Designate one of these as *Area A* and the other as *Area B*, and cut the following:

- 6 squares from Area A
- 10 squares from Area B

# Putting It Together

### Piecing

The center of Holiday Quick Quilt is pieced in smaller units designated as Units I, II, and III. To assemble Unit I, stitch two large burgundy triangles (B) on opposite sides of a plaid Area A (PA) square, as in Diagram 7-1, using ¼" seams. Add the small burgundy corner triangle (B) to complete Unit I as shown in Diagram 7-2. Press the seams to one side as suggested by the arrow in Diagram 7-2. Make two such units.

**Diagram 7-1. Unit I Piecing**

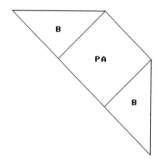

**Diagram 7-2. Completed Unit I**

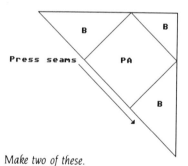

*Make two of these.*

To assemble Unit II, join one burgundy square (B), two large burgundy triangles (B), and two plaid Area B squares (PB), according to Diagram 7-3. Press the seams to one side, in the opposite direction of that indicated for Unit I (as suggested by the arrow). Make two such units.

**Diagram 7-3. Completed Unit II**

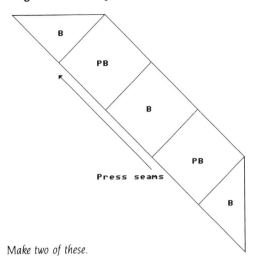

*Make two of these.*

To assemble Unit III, join two burgundy squares (B), one burgundy large triangle (B), one burgundy small triangle (B), two plaid Area A (PA) squares, and one plaid Area B (PB) square according to Diagram 7-4. Press the seams to one side, in the opposite direction of that indicated for Unit II (as suggested by the arrow in Diagram 7-4). Make two such units.

**Diagram 7-4. Completed Unit III**

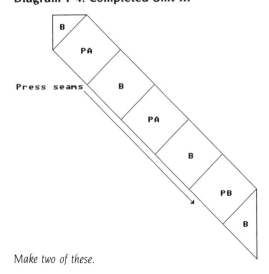

*Make two of these.*

Lay the six pieced units right side up in the diagonal arrangement shown in Diagram 7-5. Join the sections in diagonal seams, being careful to ''butterfly'' the seams at each intersection. This should happen naturally if the units have been pressed as suggested.

**Diagram 7-5. Layout of Units I, II, and III**

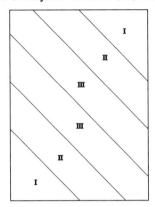

## Corner Squares and Borders

To complete each of the four corner squares, stitch four small burgundy triangles (B) to each side of a plaid Area B square (PB), as shown in Diagram 7-6, and press the seams toward the triangles.

**Diagram 7-6. Completed Corner Square**

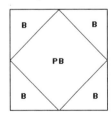

*Make four of these.*

Refer to Diagram 7-7 to complete the quilt top. First, add the two forest green (G) side borders. Then stitch a corner square to each end of the top and bottom borders, as shown in Diagram 7-8. Add these to the pieced center to complete the quilt top.

**Diagram 7-7. Completed Holiday Quick Quilt**

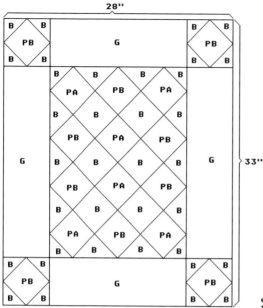

**Diagram 7-8. Piecing for Top and Bottom Borders**

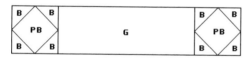

# The Finished Product

## Quilting

Place the muslin backing right side down, and smooth the batting over it. Place the pressed quilt top over the batting, right side up, and pin or baste the three layers together for quilting.

Make a quilting stencil from the star shown in Design 7-A. Suggested quilting designs are given in Diagram 7-9.

**Diagram 7-9. Suggested Quilting for Holiday Quick Quilt**

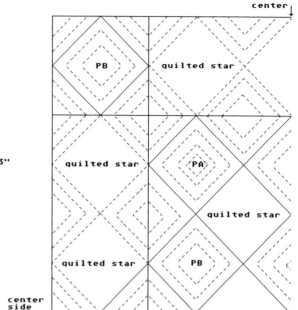

Using a soap chip or washable marking pencil to mark the following designs, and using natural-color quilting thread:

- Quilt "in the ditch" around each square and triangle; then stitch two or three smaller squares within each plaid square along selected lines in the plaid. (Area A squares and Area B squares may be quilted differently.)
- Quilt additional squares in the area where the borders meet the center pieced area, and stitch additional triangles along the outer edge of the green border.
- Quilt a star on each burgundy square (six stars) and on the green borders (four stars on each side, three stars on each end).

## Finishing

Trim the batting to ½" larger than the quilt top to allow for filler in the binding, and trim the quilt backing to match the top. Use the 1½" burgundy and green strips for binding, applying green strips along the corner squares and burgundy strips along the green side and end borders. With right sides together, stitch the binding to the quilt top in a ¼" seam and fold the binding to the back of the quilt. Turn the binding under ¼" and whipstitch it in place.

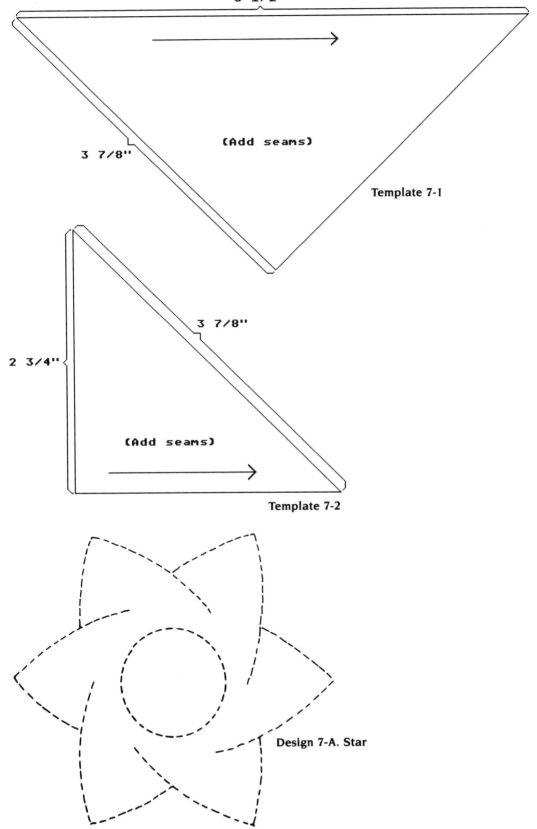

5 1/2"

(Add seams)

3 7/8"

Template 7-1

3 7/8"

2 3/4"

(Add seams)

Template 7-2

Design 7-A. Star

61

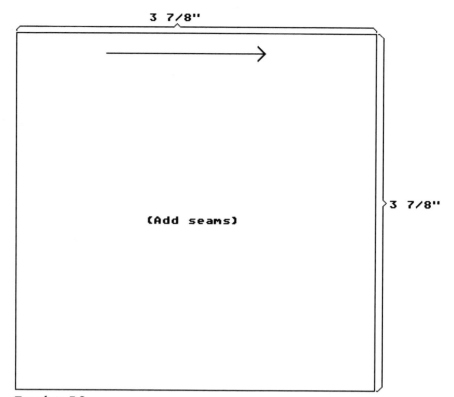

3 7/8"

3 7/8"

(Add seams)

**Template 7-3**

# Chapter 8
# Bow Tie Wall Quilt

Quilt by the author

## Remarks

The Bow Tie is a popular traditional quilt pattern. Because of the pattern's simplicity and the minimum of shapes and numbers of pieces required, it is also quick and easy to assemble. The templates used here are of fairly good size, so your piecing should go quickly.

The Bow Tie may be hung either horizontally or vertically, so you may plan your fabric layout and selection accordingly. Also, this pattern can easily be used as a crib quilt.

A variety of light, medium, and dark scraps will add interest to your design, as will a mixture of fine prints, bold prints, florals, plaids, and other fabric designs—note the variety of fabrics used in the color photograph. My earlier book, *Award-Winning Scrap Quilts*—also available through the Wallace-Homestead Book Company—is a helpful reference for selecting and utilizing scraps.

## For Starters

- Wash and press all fabrics before you begin.
- A variety of fabric scraps are needed for the bow ties—as many as 50 fabrics may be used.
- The background and border fabrics are light green and deep lavender solids.
- Blocks (a total of 18) each measure 6" square.
- The border measures 3" wide.
- Seam width is ¼".
- The finished size for the Bow Tie Wall Quilt is 31½" × 40".

## Supplies

### Quilt Top Fabric
Use 44"/45"–wide cotton or cotton/polyester blends.

*Scraps.* Choose a variety of light, medium, and dark fabrics to total about 2 yards. The number of scrap fabrics used may be as few as 3 (to make all bow ties the same) or as many as 54 (to make every bow tie and center different). The minimum scrap size is about 3" × 3" for the center of the bow and 4" × 8" for the bow ends.

*Other fabrics.* Use the following:

Light green     1¾ yards (for the background and binding)
Deep lavender  ½ yard (for the border)

## Backing
Requires 1 yard of unbleached muslin.

## Batting
Choose either crib batting (45" × 60") or a 35" × 45" piece of bonded polyester.

## Other Supplies
• Regular sewing thread to match the fabrics
• A sewing machine
• A long straightedge
• A pencil
• One spool of natural-color quilting thread
• Thread or safety pins for basting
• Soap chips or marking pencils
• Pins and quilting needles
• A large right triangle or T-square
• Scissors
• Cardboard or plastic for templates
• A hoop or frame for quilting

# Ready to Work

## Color Key
LS    Light scrap
DS    Dark scrap
G     Light green
L     Deep lavender

## Cutting
Make plastic or cardboard templates for the four bow tie pieces (Templates 1, 2, 3, and 4); note that ¼" seam allowances must be added. Be sure to indicate the grain-line arrow on each template.

Begin with the light and medium light fabric scraps (LS) and cut the following pieces:

• 9 from Template 1 (square)
• 36 (18 pairs) from Template 2 (trapezoid)

Next, cut the following pieces from the dark and medium dark scraps (DS):

• 9 from Template 1 (square)
• 36 (18 pairs) from Template 2 (trapezoid)

Cut the following pieces from the light green (G) background fabric:

• 10 from Template 3 (large triangle)
• 4 from Template 4 (small triangle)

Set the remainder of the light green fabric aside for binding.

Last, cut the following borders from the deep lavender (L) fabric:

• 2 side borders, 3½" × 34½"
• 2 end borders, 3½" × 32"

## Piecing
Gather the five pieces that constitute a bow tie unit (two light trapezoids, two dark trapezoids, and one center square). With the right sides together, join a light trapezoid to one side of the center square, as in Diagram 8-1. Likewise, add the other light trapezoid to the opposite side of the square, as in Diagram 8-2.

Finally, join the two dark trapezoids to the center square. To do this, use a pivot seam: Beginning at the outside of the unit, stitch toward the center square; next stitch along the square and then back to the outside of the trapezoid, as shown in Diagram 8-3. Press the seams away from the center square, toward the darker trapezoids.

Continue piecing until you've made 18 bow ties. Each unit will measure 6½" square without seam allowances.

**Diagram 8-1. Piecing a Bow Tie, Step 1**

*Join a light trapezoid to the center square.*

**Diagram 8-2. Piecing a Bow Tie, Step 2**

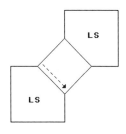

**Diagram 8-3. Step 3: Joining Dark Trapezoids to the Center Square**

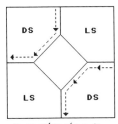

*Use a pivot seam to complete the unit.*

# Putting It Together

### Assembly of Bow Ties

At this point, lay all 18 units on a flat surface, and arrange the blocks in a format that permits maximum contrast between light and dark scraps (try several arrangements).

For the effect of light and dark gridwork, as in the Bow Tie quilt pictured in the color section of this book, place four bow tie units with the darkest fabrics coming together to form a dark octagon, as in Diagram 8-4. Fill in with additional bow ties so that light trapezoids touch the light parts of neighboring bow ties; then, when another block is added, the light trapezoids will form an octagon of light fabrics. Continue placing bow tie units with fabrics grouped to form light and dark octagons, as in Diagram 8-5. The suggested 18-block layout is shown in Diagram 8-6.

**Diagram 8-4. Bow Tie Layout for Light and Dark Gridwork Effect**

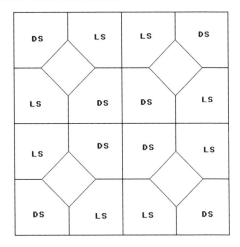

**Diagram 8-5. Pattern of Light and Dark Octagons**

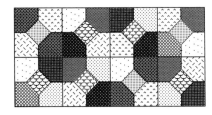

**Diagram 8-6. Suggested 18-Block Layout for Bow Tie Wall Quilt**

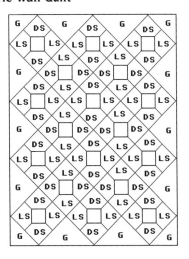

## Assembling the Center

The center of the Bow Tie Wall Quilt is assembled in smaller units designated I, II, and III. To assemble Unit I, stitch large light green triangles (G) on opposite sides of a bow tie block, as in Diagram 8-7, using ¼" seams. Add the small light green corner triangle (G) to complete Unit I, as shown in Diagram 8-8, and press the seams to one side, as suggested by the arrow in Diagram 8-8. Make two such units.

**Diagram 8-7. Unit I Assembly**

**Diagram 8-8. Completed Unit I**

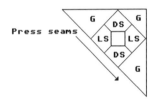

*Make two of these units.*

To assemble Unit II, stitch two large light green triangles (G) and three bow tie blocks according to Diagram 8-9. Press the seams to one side, in the opposite direction of that indicated for Unit I, as suggested by the arrow. Make two such units.

**Diagram 8-9. Completed Unit II**

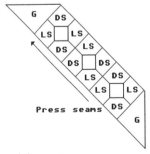

*Make two of these units.*

To assemble Unit III, join one large light green triangle (G), one small light green triangle (G), and five bow tie blocks, according to Diagram 8-10. Press the seams to one side, in the opposite direction of that indicated for Unit II, as suggested by the arrow. Make two such units.

**Diagram 8-10. Completed Unit III**

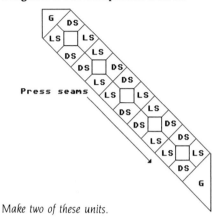

*Make two of these units.*

Lay the six pieced units right sides up in the diagonal arrangement shown in Diagram 8-11. Join the sections in diagonal seams, being careful to "butterfly" the seams at each intersection. This should happen naturally if the units have been pressed as suggested.

**Diagram 8-11. Diagonal Layout of Units I, II, and III**

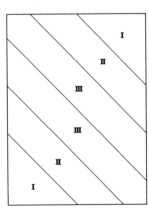

Refer to Diagram 8-12 to complete the quilt top: First add the two deep lavender (L) side borders, then the top and bottom borders.

**Diagram 8-12. Bow Tie Wall Quilt Layout Showing Borders**

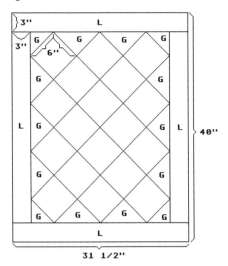

**Diagram 8-13. Suggested Quilting for Bow Tie Wall Quilt**

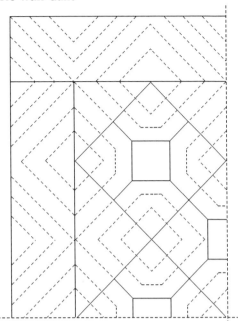

# The Finished Product

## Quilting

Place the 1 yard of muslin backing fabric right side down, and smooth the batting over it. Place the pressed top over the batting, right side up, and pin or baste the three layers together for quilting.

Suggested quilting designs are given in Diagram 8-13. Use a straightedge and a soap chip or washable marking pencil to mark the designs, and use natural-color quilting thread for quilting.

## Finishing

Trim the batting to ½" larger than the quilt top to allow for filler in the binding, and trim the quilt backing to match the top. Make 3"-wide bias strips from the remaining light green (G) fabric, and piece these strips to a length of about 5 yards. For a finished binding of about ½", fold the binding wrong sides together and attach it to the quilt front, making sure the seam goes through all five layers. Turn the binding to the back of the quilt and whipstitch it in place.

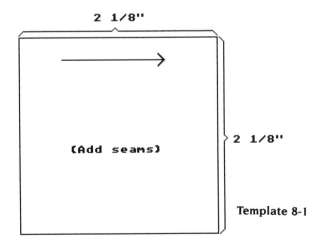

2 1/8"

2 1/8"

(Add seams)

**Template 8-1**

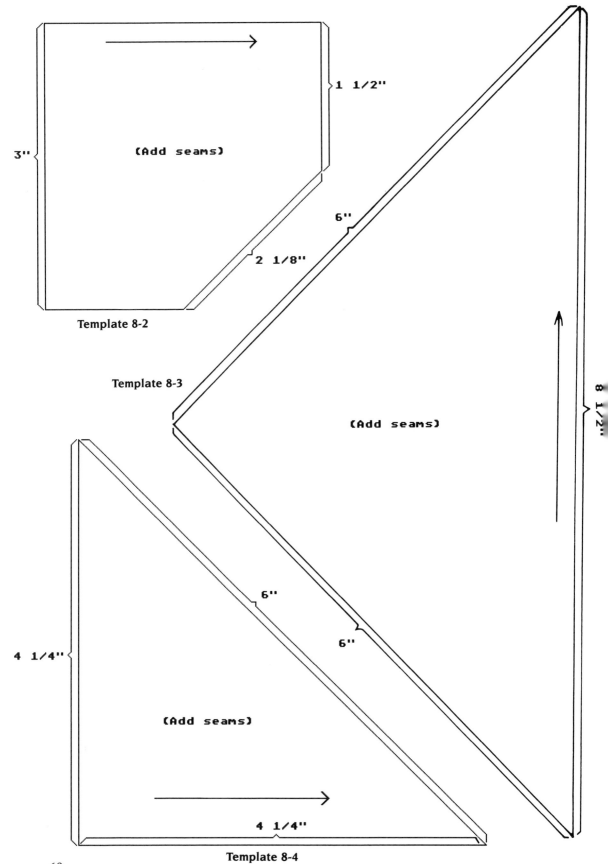

1 1/2"

3"

(Add seams)

Template 8-2

6"

2 1/8"

Template 8-3

(Add seams)

8 1/2"

6"

4 1/4"

6"

(Add seams)

4 1/4"

4 1/4"

Template 8-4

# Chapter 9
# Computer Symmetry

Quilt by Ann Ohl; design selected from the author's
*Computer Kaleidoscope* program.

## Remarks

Ann made this quilt for her son Mike, who made the decisions regarding design and color—he ran the computer program and selected his own pattern and range of colors. His personal involvement in creating this quilt made it extra special.

The assembly of Computer Symmetry is quite elementary. Although there are several shapes in the design, it isn't necessary to make any templates or patterns. Instead, all the fabrics are cut in strips of varying widths and are then pieced together and re-cut into panel designs. All the piecing can be done by machine; the cutting can be done with a rotary cutter, a mat, and a straightedge or pair of good-quality fabric scissors, and the entire top can be cut and assembled in a couple of days. After you've become familiar with this technique, you'll find it easy and efficient.

If the idea of quilt patterns generated on a home computer interests you, I recommend my book *Award-Winning Quilts, Book* II (also published by Wallace-Homestead Book Company). It includes two additional computer-designed quilts—one full-size bed quilt and one wall quilt. Both symmetrical and asymmetrical designs are explored in *Award-Winning Quilts, Book* II.

## For Starters

- Wash and press all fabrics before you begin.
- Ann's quilt uses six solid-color fabrics.
- No templates are needed.
- Most of the cutting can be done with a rotary cutter and mat.
- The inner (brown) borders measure 5" wide and the outer (blue) borders are 4" wide.
- The seam width is ¼".
- The finished size for Computer Symmetry is 82" × 90"—appropriate for a twin or full-size bed.

## Supplies

**Quilt Top Fabric**
Use 44"/45"–wide cotton or cotton/polyester blends.

| | |
|---|---|
| Ivory | 1 yard |
| Tan | 2 yards |
| Cocoa | ¾ yard |
| Country blue | 5½ yards (includes borders) |
| Brown | 1 yard |
| Dark brown | 2½ yards (borders and binding) |

## Backing
Requires 5½ yards of unbleached muslin.

## Batting
Use a 90" × 108" (queen size) piece of bonded polyester.

## Other Supplies
• Regular sewing thread to match the fabrics
• A sewing machine
• A long straightedge
• A pencil
• Three spools of dark brown quilting thread
• Thread or safety pins for basting
• Soap chips or marking pencils
• Pins and quilting needles
• Scissors
• A rotary cutter and mat
• A hoop or frame for quilting

# Ready to Work

## Color Key
I   Ivory
T   Tan
C   Cocoa
CB  Country blue
B   Brown
DB  Dark brown

## Cutting
Begin with the 1-yard piece of ivory (I) fabric. Fold it in half lengthwise, right sides together, and secure it with pins. (If you're using solid-color fabrics, there's no right or wrong side of the fabric for all practical purposes.) Mark and cut two narrow strips, each 2¾" wide, across the folded fabric, as in Diagram 9-1. Then cut along the fold at the end of each strip. You'll have four 2¾" × 22" strips. Strip units will be about 22" long, depending on the exact width of your folded fabric.

**Diagram 9-1. Layout for Ivory (I)**

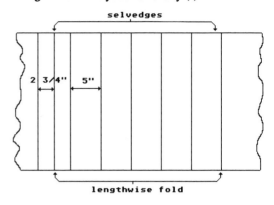

Next, mark five medium strips, each 5" wide, on the folded fabric. Cut along the fold at the end of each strip. You will have ten 5"-wide strips.

Continue with the tan (T) fabric (2 yards). Fold it in half lengthwise as described and then mark and cut strips according to Diagram 9-2. Remember to cut across the folded ends as well. Cut the following pieces from the folded tan fabric:

• 4 strips, 2¾" wide
• 3 strips, 5" wide
• 1 strip, 7¼" wide
• 1 strip, 9½" wide
• 1 strip, 14" wide (After cutting the end fold, trim one strip to 11¾".)

Next, cut a 9½"-wide strip from the cocoa (C) fabric (¾ yard), according to Diagram 9-3. After cutting the end fold, trim one piece to 7¼".

**Diagram 9-2. Layout for Tan (T)**

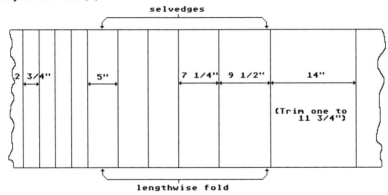

**Diagram 9-4. Layout for Country Blue (CB)**

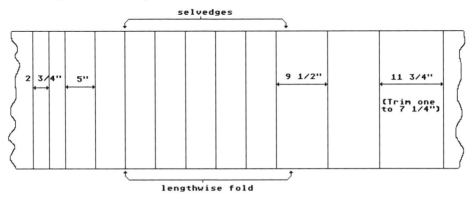

**Diagram 9-3. Layout for Cocoa (C)**

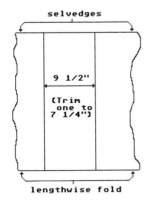

- 2 strips, 2¾" wide
- 7 strips, 5" wide
- 2 strips, 9½" wide
- 1 strip, 11¾" wide (After cutting the end fold, trim one strip to 7¼".)

From the 1 yard of brown (B) fabric, cut the following strips as shown in Diagram 9-5:

- 4 strips, 2¾" wide
- 2 strips, 5" wide

Next, cut a 2¾-yard piece from the country blue (CB) fabric, label it to be used for borders, and set it aside. From the remaining CB fabric, cut the following strips (as shown in Diagram 9-4):

**Diagram 9-5. Layout for Brown (B)**

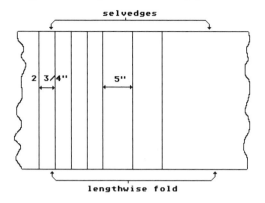

## Piecing

Begin with row 1 and gather the required strips from top to bottom (row 1 will have seven strips), using Diagram 9-6 as your color guide. Mark this pile of strips *row* 1 and set it aside. Likewise, gather the strips for the remaining seven rows (using Diagram 9-6) and label them accordingly.

    Row 1: Seven strips
    Row 2: Eight strips
    Row 3: Nine strips
    Row 4: Eight strips
    Row 5: Nine strips
    Row 6: Seven strips
    Row 7: Six strips
    Row 8: Eight strips

**Diagram 9-6. Piecing for Rows 1–8 (One-Fourth of Quilt Top)**

| Row # 1 | 2 | 3 | 4 | 5 | 6 | 7 | 8 |
|---|---|---|---|---|---|---|---|
| CB |  | CB | T | T |  |  | I |
|  | T | T |  |  | CB | CB |  |
|  |  |  | B | CB |  |  | CB |
|  |  | CB | T |  |  |  | I |
| T | CB |  | B | T | T | T |  |
|  | I | T | T |  |  | CB | CB |
| CB | B |  | B | CB | CB |  |  |
|  | T | B |  | B |  | C |  |
| T |  | CB | I | T |  |  | T |
| CB | CB |  |  | CB | C |  | I |
|  | B |  |  | T | T | CB |  |
| I | I | CB | T | CB | B |  | CB |
| CB | CB | I |  |  | I | B | B |

Gather and label the strips for each row to ensure you have the correct number, size, and color of strips for each row (using Diagram 9-6 as your guide) before you proceed with assembling them. If there is a discrepancy at this point, cut any additional required pieces you will need. There will be a few extra cut strips to add to your scrap bag.

With the right sides together, pin the long sides of the strips of row 1 as shown in Diagram 9-7. Piece the strips so that one end of the row is flush, which will leave the other end of the row uneven (Diagram 9-7). Join using ¼" seams, and set row 1 aside. Likewise, join the strips of the remaining eight rows. Press the seams of all odd-numbered rows up and the seams of all even-numbered rows down.

**Diagram 9-7. Row 1 Piecing**

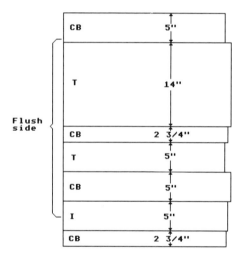

Lay the assembled row 1 on a flat surface or cutting mat. Using a straightedge, mark a line along the flush side and mark four more lines at 4½" intervals, resulting in four columns, as shown in Diagram 9-8. Carefully cut along the marked lines—there will be some waste at the uneven side. Label these four strips *row* 1 and set them aside.

Repeat by marking and cutting the remaining seven rows in 4½" columns.

### Diagram 9-8. Row 1 Cutting Lines

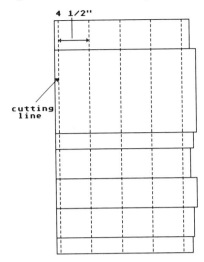

4 1/2"

cutting
line

# Putting It Together

## Assembly of Rows

Assemble a quarter section of the quilt by joining row 1 to row 2, and so on through row 8, as in Diagram 9-9. Repeat for the other three quarter sections of the quilt. Press all seams to one side.

### Diagram 9-9. Layout for Computer Symmetry Showing Assembled Quarter Sections and Borders

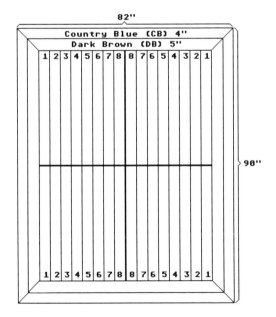

82"

Country Blue (CB)  4"
Dark Brown (DB)  5"

| 1 | 2 | 3 | 4 | 5 | 6 | 7 | 8 | 8 | 7 | 6 | 5 | 4 | 3 | 2 | 1 |

90"

| 1 | 2 | 3 | 4 | 5 | 6 | 7 | 8 | 8 | 7 | 6 | 5 | 4 | 3 | 2 | 1 |

At this point you may proceed to make the quilt that Ann designed, or you may want to experiment with alternative arrangements of the four quarter sections. Lay the four sections on a large flat surface and turn each section end-for-end, or exchange with other sections to see various symmetrical and asymmetrical designs. If you have the book *Award-Winning Quilts, Book II*, refer to the two computer-pattern sections for additional ideas.

After you've selected your design, join the four quarter sections to complete the central area of the quilt (about 64" × 72") as in Diagram 9-9.

### Assembly of Borders

Cut the two sets of borders (measurements include allowances for seams and mitering).

From the 2½-yard piece of dark brown (DB) fabric, cut:
• 2 side borders, 5½" × 82½"
• 2 end borders, 5½" × 74½"

(Save the remaining fabric for binding.)

From the 2¾-yard piece of country blue (CB) fabric, cut:
• 2 side borders, 4½" × 90½"
• 2 end borders, 4½" × 82½"

Add the borders to the central design, beginning with the 5" dark brown (DB), inner border. Last, add the 4" country blue (CB), outer border. Miter all corners. (See Diagram 9-9.)

# The Finished Product

### Quilting

Cut the 5½ yards of unbleached muslin backing fabric into two 2¾-yard lengths, leaving one piece intact. Split the other piece into two 22" panels and stitch to each side of the intact piece. Press the seams to the outside.

Place the backing right side down, and smooth the batting over it. Place the pressed quilt top over the batting, right side up, and pin or baste the three layers together for quilting.

With a straightedge and soap chip or washable marking pencil, mark the following suggested quilting lines (shown in Diagram 9-10):

- Elongated x's on the ivory (I)
- Diagonal parallel lines on the tan (T)
- Brickwork lines on the cocoa (C)
- Horizontal parallel lines on the country blue (CB)
- Vertical parallel lines on the brown (B)

Use dark brown quilting thread.

**Diagram 9-10. Suggested Quilting for Computer Symmetry**

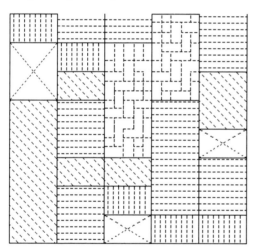

## Finishing

Trim the batting to ½" larger than the quilt top to allow for filler in the binding, and trim the quilt backing to match the top. Make 3"-wide continuous bias binding from the remaining dark brown (DB) fabric. For a finished binding of about ½", fold the binding wrong sides together and attach it to the quilt front, making sure the seam goes through all five layers. Turn the binding to the back of the quilt and whipstitch it in place.

# Chapter 10
# Little Red Schoolhouse

Quilt by Pat Simonsen

## Remarks

This popular little schoolhouse pattern is attractive in a combination of bright colors. Pat has adapted the usual traditional patterns into a design of her own that features dual chimneys and paired windows. Her mixture of red schoolhouse prints, blue sky fabrics, and green grass panels is cheerful and refreshing.

In addition to the variety of fabrics used, each schoolhouse has its own quilted roof design—these 16 designs are included in the pattern section.

Little Red Schoolhouse can be pieced quickly and easily on the sewing machine. If you're working with new fabrics (rather than scraps) and you're using the same fabrics throughout, you may take advantage of additional shortcuts such as strip-piecing the window, sky, and door units. The innovative "quick piecer" can apply several shortcut methods to Little Red Schoolhouse.

To simplify cutting and piecing, some templates have been slightly altered from the pictured project. Please read through all instructions before you begin.

## For Starters

- Wash and press all fabrics before you begin.
- Pat's Little Red Schoolhouse is made of 16 blocks, each 8" square.
- Each block uses five fabrics and has 19 pieces.
- The schoolhouses may be made from scraps (as pictured) or from new coordinated fabrics. Measurements and suggestions are given for both methods.
- The dark blue latticework is 2" wide.
- Seam width is ¼".
- The finished size for Little Red Schoolhouse is 42" × 42".

## Supplies

**Quilt Top Fabric**
Use 44"/45"–wide cotton or cotton/polyester blends.

| | New Fabric | or | Scraps |
|---|---|---|---|
| Red (house and chimneys) | 1 yard | | 16 pieces, each at least 10" X 10" |
| Blue (roof and door) | ½ yard | | 16 pieces, each at least 8" X 10" |
| Coordinating blue (sky) | ⅜ yard | | 16 pieces, each at least 6" X 6" |
| Yellow (windows) | ⅛ yard | | 16 pieces, each at least 4" X 4" |
| Green (grass) | ¼ yard | | 16 pieces, each at least 2" X 10" |
| Dark blue (lattice/borders) | 1⅜ yard | | 1⅜ yard |

## Backing
Requires 1½ yards of unbleached muslin.

## Binding
Use ¾ yard of red.

## Batting
Choose either crib batting (45" X 60") or a 45" X 45" piece of bonded polyester.

## Other Supplies
- Regular sewing thread to match the fabrics
- A sewing machine
- A long straightedge
- A pencil
- One spool of red quilting thread
- Thread or safety pins for basting
- Soap chips or marking pencils
- Pins and quilting needles
- Scissors
- Plastic or cardboard for templates
- A hoop or frame for quilting
- Optional: a rotary cutter and cutting mat

# Ready to Work

## Color Key
R   Red
B   Blue
CB  Coordinating blue
Y   Yellow
G   Green
DB  Dark blue

## Cutting
Make cardboard or plastic templates of the eight shapes (10-A through 10-H), noting the grain-line arrows. Also note that seam allowances are *not* included on the patterns.

For machine piecing, be sure to add ¼" seam allowances on all sides of each template.

Beginning with the red (R) scraps, cut the following for *each* schoolhouse:

- Template 10-A   6 pieces
- Template 10-C   2 pieces
- Template 10-D   2 pieces
- Template 10-F   1 piece

(If you're using the *same* red fabric for each block, multiply these numbers by 16—cut 96 from Template 10-A, 32 from 10-C, 32 from 10-D, and 16 from 10-F.)

Next, for the roof and door, cut the following from each blue (B) scrap:

- Template 10-B   1 piece
- Template 10-G   1 piece

(Again, if you're using the same blue in each block, multiply these numbers by 16—cut 16 from 10-B and 16 from 10-G.)

Continue with the coordinating blue (CB) scraps. Cut the following pieces for the sky:

- Template 10-C   1 piece
- Template 10-H   2 pieces (1 reverse)

(Or cut 16 of 10-C and 32 of 10-H—16 reverse—if using the same fabric throughout.)

Next, cut the yellow (Y) scraps for the windows:

- Template 10-A   2 pieces

(Or cut 32 of 10-A if using the same fabric throughout.)

Next, cut the green (G) pieces for grass:

• Template 10-E  1 piece

(Or cut 16 of 10-E if using the same green throughout.)

From the 1⅜-yard piece of dark blue (DB), cut the following (¼" seam allowances included):

• 12 short strips, 2½" × 8½"
• 3 cross-lattices, 2½" × 38½"
• 4 borders, 2½" × 42½"

# Putting It Together

### Piecing

Refer to Diagram 10-1 for the arrangement of the schoolhouse pieces. Lay the cut pieces for one block (a total of 19 pieces) right sides up. Use ¼" seams and piece in the order of steps 1–7 below.

**Diagram 10-1. Piecing Arrangement for Little Red Schoolhouse**

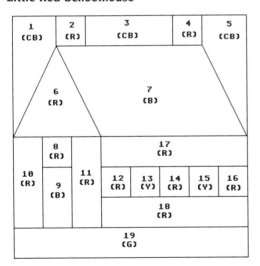

Step 1. Join pieces 1, 2, 3, 4, and 5 as shown in Diagram 10-2. At the points marked X, leave the ¼" seam allowance free so you can insert the roof section.

**Diagram 10-2. Step 1: Sky/Chimney Section**

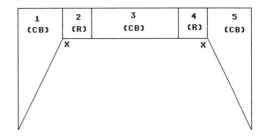

Step 2. Join pieces 6 and 7 as in Diagram 10-3.

**Diagram 10-3. Step 2: Roof Section**

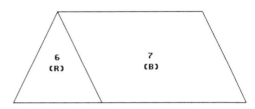

Step 3. Pin these two sections together (pieces 1–7) and join them in pivot seams, as shown by the arrows in Diagram 10-4.

**Diagram 10-4. Step 3: Upper (Roof) Section**

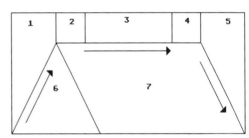

Step 4. Stitch piece 8 to piece 9 and then add pieces 10 and 11, as in Diagram 10-5.

**Diagram 10-5. Step 4: Door Section**

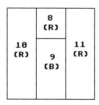

*Step* 5. Stitch pieces 12, 13, 14, 15, and 16 together; then add piece 17 and piece 18, as shown in Diagram 10-6.

**Diagram 10-6. Step 5: Window Section**

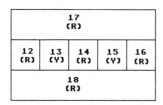

*Step* 6. Join these two sections together (pieces 8–18); then add the grass piece (19) as shown in Diagram 10-7.

**Diagram 10-7. Step 6: Lower Section**

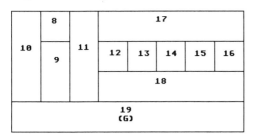

*Step* 7. Join the lower section to the roof section to complete the block as pictured in Diagram 10-1.

## Latticework

Arrange a panel of four schoolhouse blocks and three dark blue (DB) short lattice strips as shown in Diagram 10-8, and stitch using ¼" seams. Make three similar panels.

**Diagram 10-8. Row 1 Piecing**

| school-house | DB | school-house | DB | school-house | DB | school-house |
|---|---|---|---|---|---|---|

Place a cross-lattice (38½" X 2½") between each row and stitch, using Diagram 10-9 as your guide. Add the top, bottom, and side borders, using mitered corners.

**Diagram 10-9. Layout for Little Red Schoolhouse Showing Latticework and Borders**

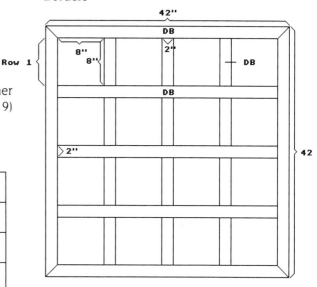

# The Finished Product

### Quilting

Place the 1½ yards of muslin backing right side down, and smooth the batting over it. Place the pressed quilt top over the batting, right side up, and pin or baste the three layers together for quilting.

Quilt "in the ditch" around the structural parts of the house and along all borders. Quilt straight lines on each lattice and border about ½" from the seams.

Add decorative quilting on each rooftop. Pat's 16 roof-quilting designs are included in the pattern section, or you can make your own quilted roof designs to reflect the pattern in your roof fabrics.

## Finishing

Trim the batting to ½" larger than the quilt top to allow for filler in the binding, and trim the quilt backing to match the top. Make 3"-wide continuous bias binding from the ¾-yard piece of red fabric. For a finished binding about ½" wide, fold the binding wrong sides together and attach it to the quilt front, making sure the seam goes through all five layers. Turn the binding to the back of the quilt and whipstitch it in place.

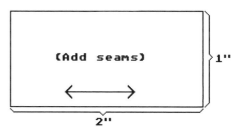

(Add seams)

1"

2"

**Template 10-B**

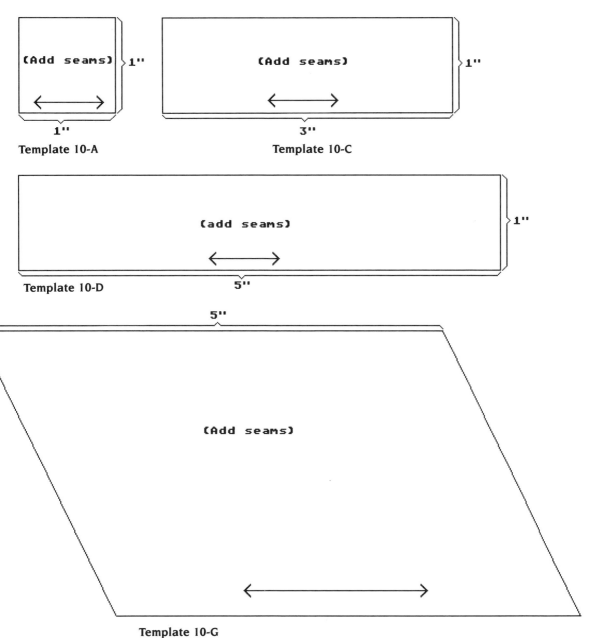

(Add seams)

1"

1"

**Template 10-A**

(Add seams)

1"

3"

**Template 10-C**

(add seams)

1"

5"

**Template 10-D**

5"

(Add seams)

**Template 10-G**

79

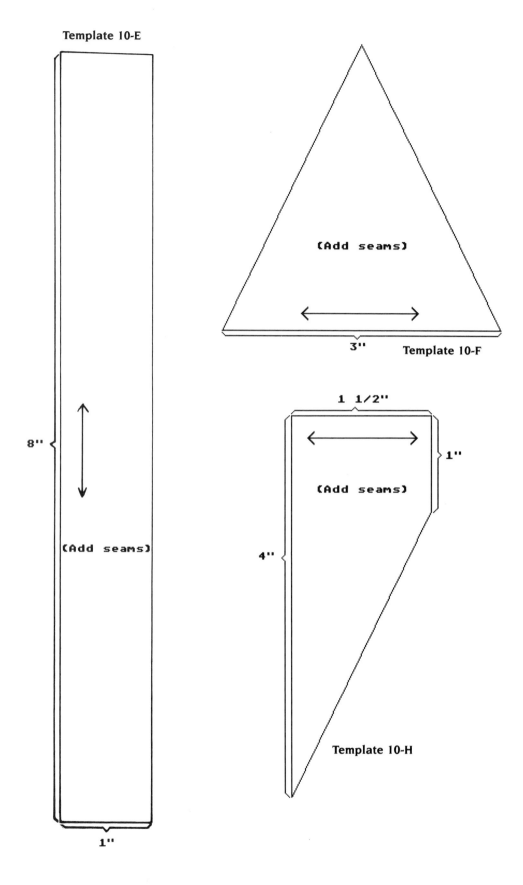

**Template 10-E**

8"

(Add seams)

1"

**Template 10-F**

(Add seams)

3"

1 1/2"

1"

(Add seams)

4"

**Template 10-H**

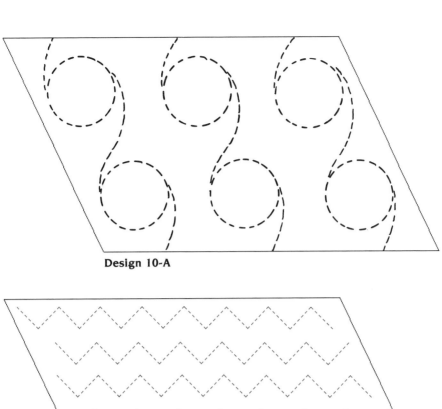

**Design 10-A**

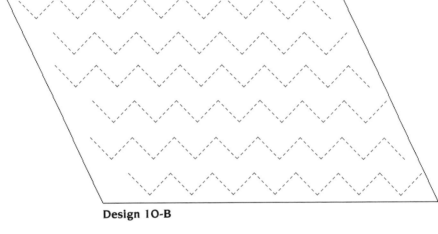

**Design 1O-B**

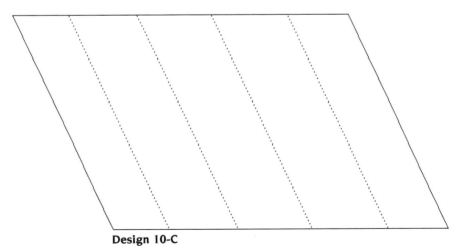

**Design 10-C**

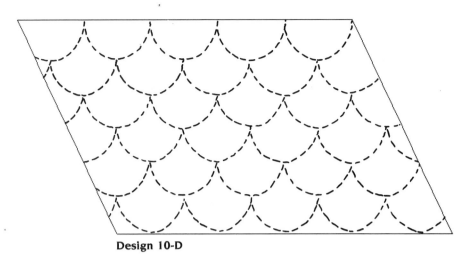

**Design 10-D**

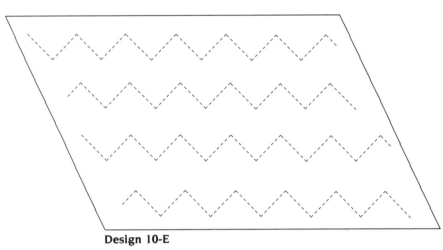

**Design 10-E**

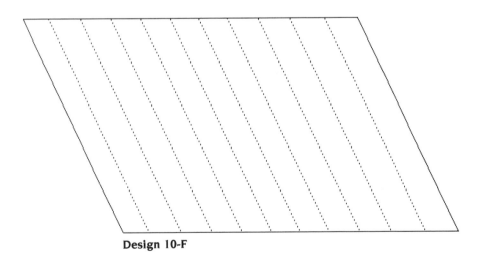

**Design 10-F**

82

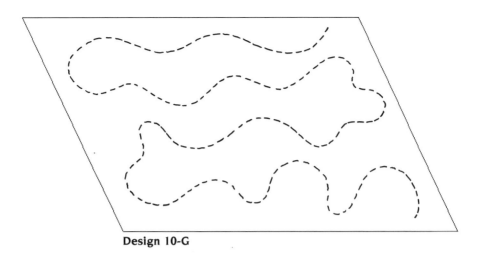

**Design 10-G**

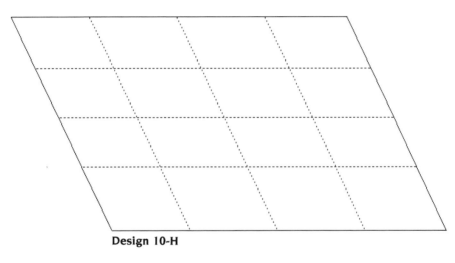

**Design 10-H**

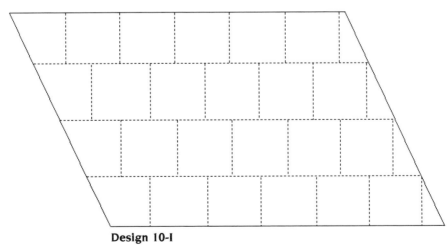

**Design 10-I**

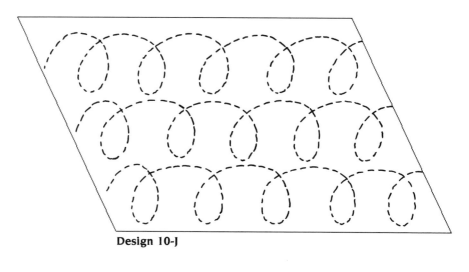

**Design 10-J**

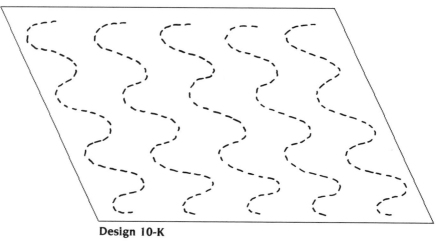

**Design 10-K**

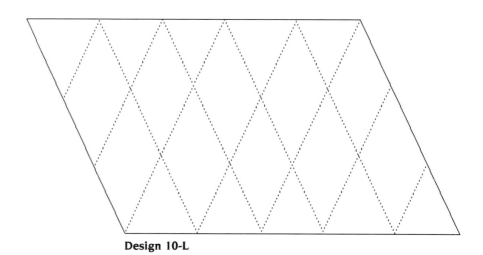

**Design 10-L**

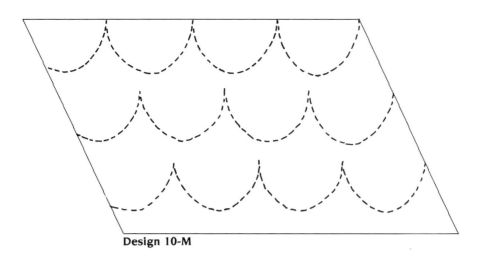

**Design 10-M**

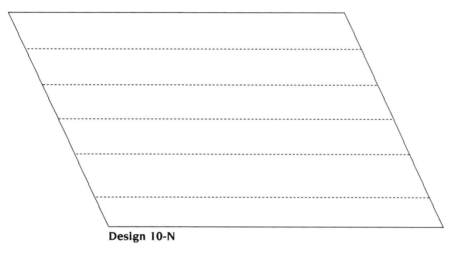

**Design 10-N**

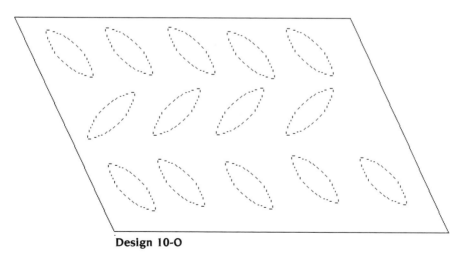

**Design 10-O**

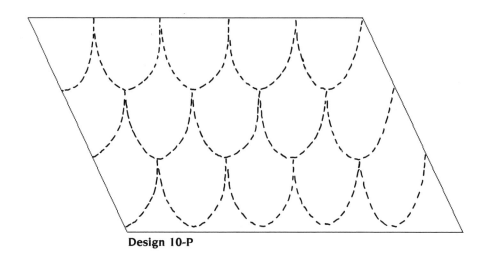

**Design 10-P**

# Appendix
# How to Make Tandem-Pieced Triangles

Tandem-piecing methods have been explored and explained in quilting books and periodicals for more than ten years. The techniques have been called by various names, among them *tandem piecing, half-a-square triangles, fast-sewn half-square triangles, quickie-piece method,* and *sandwich piecing.* These terms refer to the same basic four-step process of:

1. Marking a grid of squares and triangles on the wrong side of a piece of fabric.
2. Pinning that piece together with a second fabric, right sides together.
3. Stitching along the diagonal sewing lines.
4. And finally, cutting the fabric pieces into squares and then triangle combination units.

The result is pieced squares composed of two half-square triangles, as shown in Diagram A-1. These are referred to as *combination units.*

**Diagram A-1. Combination Unit of Half-Square Triangles**

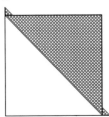

## Seam Allowances

Beyond the four steps just mentioned, there is some disagreement regarding the best procedures to use. For instance, recommended seam allowances vary—some suggest ½", while others say ¼". I suggest you consider the advantages and disadvantages of each and then make your own choice.

**Using ½" Seams**
Advantages:
- Grid lines and stitching lines fall on the ¼" or ½" marks on the ruler, which are more familiar and therefore easier to mark.
- ½" lines are easier to sew, especially for the vision-impaired.

Disadvantages:
- A greater percentage of fabric is wasted in the seams. (The seams could be trimmed later, but this is a tedious and time-consuming project.)
- Quilting design versatility is restricted because quilting possibilities are eliminated in most of the areas within ½" of the seam lines.
- ½" seams create more difficult-to-quilt territory (thicker seam areas).

## Using ¼" Seams

Advantages:
- There is less fabric waste.
- A ¼" seam lends itself well to traditional ¼" outline quilting.
- It may be easier to stitch for those accustomed to ¼" seams.

Disadvantages:
- Grids are more difficult to mark with accuracy: ⅛" increments are less familiar and more difficult to find on measuring devices, and are more likely to result in error. (Common marking intervals are 3⅜", 4⅞", and so on.)
- There is less tolerance for error when you're using ¼" seams.

The patterns in this book use *both* seam widths: Some are ½", others are ¼". The seam allowance for each quilt is specified in the second section of each chapter under "For Starters," and is respecified in the directions and accompanying illustrations.

Whether you decide to use ¼" or ½" seams, accuracy is of utmost importance. If you're unable to "eye" the exact measurement, I suggest you mark *both* stitching lines. You can do this quite efficiently using a pencil and any quilter's ruler that has the ¼"- or ½"-line increments.

# Marking Intervals for Tandem Piecing

The *size* of marking grids is also specified in each pattern. The formula and procedure for determining the marking intervals is given below. You can use this to apply to other tandem-pieced projects or if you prefer to change the seam width specified in the pattern.

### Formula A: Using ½" Seams
First, determine the finished size of the combination unit (two half-square triangles), as shown in Diagram A-2.

**Diagram A-2. Finished Measurement of a Combination Unit**

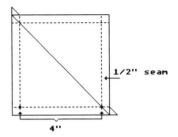

Add 1¾" to this measurement. For example, if you want 4" finished combination units, use a marking interval of 5¾" (4" + 1¾" = 5¾").

Table A-1 will help you determine marking intervals for using ½" seams.

**Table A-1. Marking Intervals for ½" Seams**

| Finished Units | Interval |
|---|---|
| 2" | 3¾" |
| 2½" | 4¼" |
| 3" | 4¾" |
| 3½" | 5¼" |
| 4" | 5¾" |
| 4½" | 6¼" |
| 5" | 6¾" |
| 5½" | 7¼" |
| 6" | 7¾" |

### Formula B: Using ¼" Seams
A similar procedure is followed for ¼" seams; the only difference is the *amount* added—⅞" rather than 1¾"—to the finished measurement of the combination units. For example, for a 4" finished combination unit, use a marking interval of 4⅞" (4" + ⅞" = 4⅞").

Table A-2 will help you determine marking intervals when using ¼" seams.

## Table A-2. Marking Intervals for ¼" Seams

| Finished Units | Interval |
|---|---|
| 2" | 2⅞" |
| 2½" | 3⅜" |
| 3" | 3⅞" |
| 3½" | 4⅜" |
| 4" | 4⅞" |
| 4½" | 5⅜" |
| 5" | 5⅞" |
| 5½" | 6⅜" |
| 6" | 6⅞" |

# Stitching Methods

Quiltmakers also disagree on the best stitching methods for tandem-pieced triangles. Two methods frequently appear in books—I call them the *diagonal* method and the *maze* method.

## Diagonal Method

The diagonal method is shown in Diagrams A-3 and A-4. Proponents of this method agree that it is less complicated to mark and stitch. Some suggest the stitching should all be in the same direction to avoid puckering (as illustrated by the arrows in Diagram A-3).

**Diagram A-3. Diagonal Method of *Uniform* Stitching**

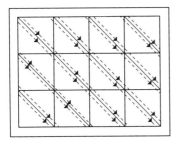

Others suggest stitching alternate rows in opposite directions (according to the arrows in Diagram A-4) for more efficient handling of the fabric and to prevent the fabric from stretching out of shape.

**Diagram A-4. Diagonal Method of *Alternate* Stitching**

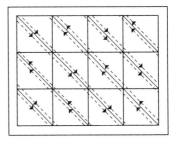

The diagonal method is somewhat tedious because it calls for frequent starts and stops, such as lifting up the sewing machine needle to cross the corners of adjacent squares. Some suggest sewing across these corners anyway and ripping out this small portion of stitched seam.

## Maze Method

The maze stitching method is shown in Diagram A-5. Proponents of this method point to its efficiency. It requires few starts and stops and, in an ideal situation, only one start and stop may be required—you may stitch in one continuous motion.

**Diagram A-5. Maze Method of Stitching**

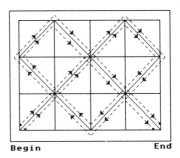

Begin                                    End

Some suggest that because you eventually stitch in all four directions, the maze method also reduces fabric distortion. One author further suggests that placement of one of the fabrics at a 90-degree angle to the other (one piece on the crosswise grain, the other on the lengthwise grain) will minimize stretching.

Stitching directions for the tandem-pieced quilts in this book recommend the maze method. Complete illustrations for marking and stitching are included.

# General Directions for Tandem Piecing

*Step* 1. Begin by cutting a large piece of each of two selected fabrics. The pieces should be large enough for marking several squares. (Fabric sizes are given for each pattern in the book.)

*Step* 2. Mark a grid of squares on the wrong side of one of the fabric pieces, as specified in the pattern or according to the procedure outlined above. In the example in Diagram A-6, ½" seams will be used and the squares are marked at 6" intervals for finished 4¼" combination units (4¼" + 1¾" = 6"). Be sure to leave some fabric clearance all the way around.

**Diagram A-6. Marking Grid for Squares**

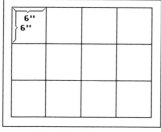

*Mark on **wrong** side of the fabric.*

*Step* 3. Mark diagonal lines from corner to corner through each square as shown in Diagram A-7, which shows the maze method of stitching.

**Diagram A-7. Marking Grid for Triangles**

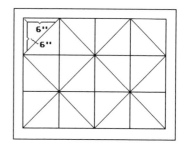

*Step* 4. Pin the marked fabric piece to the second, unmarked fabric piece, right sides together. Use one pin in each triangle.

*Step* 5. Stitch on both sides of each diagonal line ½" from the line, as shown in Diagram A-8. Begin in one corner and follow a continuous path, as illustrated by the arrows.

**Diagram A-8. Stitching Lines**

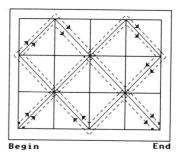

*Stitching lines shown are the **maze** method.*

*Step* 6. Cut into squares, following all straight lines. (You will have 12 squares, each with 6" sides.) Then cut each square into two triangles, following the solid diagonal lines. (You will have 24 combination units.)

*Step* 7. Press the seams to one side, toward the darker fabric, and trim the excess fabric at the corners, as shown in Diagram A-9.

**Diagram A-9. Combination Unit Before Trimming Corners**

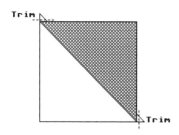

*Step* 8. You are now ready to arrange the tandem-pieced units into the design of your choice.

# Bibliography

Florence, Judy. *Award-Winning Quilts and How to Make Them.* Lombard, Illinois: Wallace-Homestead Book Company, 1986.

——. *Award-Winning Quilts, Book II.* Lombard, Illinois: Wallace-Homestead Book Company, 1986.

——. *Award-Winning Scrap Quilts.* Greensboro, North Carolina: Wallace-Homestead Book Company, 1987.

Hughes, Trudie. *Template-Free Quiltmaking.* Bothell, Washington: That Patchwork Place, Inc., 1986.

——. *More Template-Free Quiltmaking.* Bothell, Washington: That Patchwork Place, Inc., 1987.

Johannah, Barbara. *Half Square Triangles.* Lafayette, California: C & T Publishing, 1987.

——. *The Quick Quiltmaking Handbook.* Lafayette, California: C & T Publishing, 1979.

Malone, Maggie. *Quilting Shortcuts.* New York: Sterling Publishing Co., Inc., 1986.

Martin, Nancy J. *Pieces of the Past.* Bothell, Washington: That Patchwork Place, Inc., 1986.

Nephew, Sara. *Quilts from a Different Angle.* Bothell, Washington: That Patchwork Place, Inc., 1986.

Risinger, Hettie. *Innovative Machine Patchwork Piecing.* New York: Sterling Publishing Co., Inc., 1983.

# About the Author

Judy Florence has been making quilts for 15 years, and has been teaching quiltmaking for the past 10 years. She is a popular instructor at workshops in the upper Midwest and across the United States.

*Award-Winning Quick Quilts* is the fourth title in her series of books featuring award-winning quilt patterns and step-by-step instructions. Her first three books, *Award-Winning Quilts and How to Make Them*; *Award-Winning Quilts, Book II*; and *Award-Winning Scrap Quilts*, are all available from Wallace-Homestead Book Company.

Judy's current quilting interests include working with unusual fabrics, fabric mixture designs, and contemporary interpretations of traditional patterns. Her favorite part of quilting is the ''people'' part. She enjoys working on friendship quilts and helping her ten-year-old son learn to quilt.

When not involved with quilting, Judy can be found doing ''family'' things with her husband and two sons. The Florences, who reside in Eau Claire, Wisconsin, all enjoy music, get-togethers with international students, reading, and traveling abroad.